Engaging Children's Minds:
The Project Approach

Lilian G. Katz
University of Illinois
Urbana-Champaign

Sylvia C. Chard
College of St. Paul & St. Mary
Cheltenham, England

ABLEX PUBLISHING CORPORATION
NORWOOD, NEW JERSEY

Tenth Printing 1994

Printed in the United States of America

Library of Congress Cataloging-in-Publication Data

Katz, Lilian.
    Engaging children's minds : the project approach / Lilian G. Katz,
Sylvia C. Chard.
        p.   cm.
    Bibliography: p.
    Includes index.
    ISBN 0-89391-534-3.   ISBN 0-89391-543-2 (pbk.)
    1. Project method in teaching.   2. Early childhood education.
I. Chard, Sylvia C.   II. Title.   III. Series.
LB1027.43.K38 1988
371.3'6—dc19   88-8189

Ablex Publishing Corporation
355 Chestnut Street
Norwood, New Jersey 07648

Table of Contents

Foreword

To attempt a foreword to *Engaging Children's Minds: The Project Approach* is a humbling experience. In these days, when the pendulum has swung so far toward mechanistic trivia in the educational process, this book offers a refreshing approach. In our desire to make education uniform in this country, we have almost forgotten the true aims of education, especially as they concern our youngest citizens. The conclusions of the authors that "compelling evidence to support our views is needed" is far too modest, for Katz and Chard have not been content to introduce *the project method.* They have presented a method for teaching young children in such a way that the outcomes result in enriched human beings, socially, intellectually, and emotionally.

The plan is buttressed by sound and thorough research in many interrelated areas: normative and dynamic dimensions of development, learning theory, motivation, and communication. At a time when the United States appears to be losing the essential characteristics of appropriate early childhood curriculum, *the project approach* could be an effective deterrent to the "first grade push" in kindergarten and throughout the primary grades. Katz and Chard's approach is both innovative and resourceful.

The emphasis placed on the development of social competence of young children by suggesting that they learn by interacting with their own first-hand experiences and with their real environment is not a new idea. However, this book is a much needed reminder that workbooks, patterns, and cutting and tracing lines is largely a waste of children's time. More importantly, such activities are teaching the five-year-old that school is a dull place, having little in common with real life. It is not accidental that many children's zest for "going to school" at five years has been replaced, at age eight or ten, with boredom and with the children separating school hours from after school hours "when we can really live."

Engaging Children's Minds: The Project Approach offers the inexperienced teacher all of the examples needed to trigger the imagination. This is further strengthened by the presentation of various steps in implementing the project from beginning to conclusion.

If I may be allowed a personal note—I began teaching when the ideas of progressive education were flourishing. Teaching in those days was exciting and challenging, for the *teacher's mind had to be engaged along with the children's.* The outcomes of such collaboration were unpredictable and therefore the process of learning was inherently attractive to young minds. The young seek novelty. They respond to the new and innovative. There's no better way, also, for keeping the mature mind growing. Therefore, my response to this book is: *it's about time!* We need to get back in touch with the reality of the young children we teach. How auspicious that this book is appearing now, authored by such prestigious individuals as Katz and Chard!

Mary B. Lane
Professor Emerita
San Francisco State University

Preface

A class of first graders settled down for the morning assignment. Each child was to trace the outline of a maple leaf around a template onto green or yellow construction paper. They were then to cut out the leaf, draw a face on it, glue a popsicle stick to it, and use it as a puppet in a play intended to celebrate autumn and its colorful leaves.

In another class each kindergartner has cut from a ditto sheet six small, square drawings depicting the story of the Three Little Pigs. Their assignment was to paste each of the six pictures on construction paper according to the order of the story. Most seemed to place their pictures in the correct order, though several placed them upside down. Many seemed more absorbed in the properties of the glue than in the story sequence.

The activities described are not unusual. They reflect the prevailing views of their teachers that young children should be provided a mixture of creative and reading-readiness activities. Although the children in both classes pursued their activities with moderate interest, one of the girls cutting out her maple leaf turned to her neighbor and said, "You know what? This is really dumb. But my Mum will love it!" We can only speculate about the basis of her evaluation of the task.

To be sure, young children's judgments of appropriate activities are not a reliable guide to educational planning. However, it seems to us that current practice in the early years of schooling is too heavily dominated by the kinds of mindless—though harmless—activities described in the observations above. We suggest that young children should have activities that engage their minds fully in the quest for knowledge, understanding, and skill. Specifically, it is our view that the project approach described in this book provides a context in which all aspects of children's minds can be engaged, challenged, and enriched.

While most of our teaching experience has been in the United States and Great Britain, we have also worked with colleagues in other parts of the world. Although each country—indeed, each locality—has unique problems and conditions, many concerns are universal. Our experience suggests that the project approach to early childhood education can be implemented in virtually all localities.

In the descriptions and explanations of project work that follow, we have attempted to take into account the diverse conditions and varied situations in which teachers work. However, because the application of the project approach has a longer history and is most extensive in Great Britain than elsewhere, many of the examples are drawn from there. Nevertheless, we have attempted to select examples that readers can adapt to their own situations. References to underlying principles relevant to the project approach are included to help teachers judge for themselves how to adapt the approach to situations that are different from those we know best.

A NOTE ABOUT TERMS AND CONTEXTS

Early Childhood Settings

This book is addressed to teachers who work in settings known by a variety of names: preschools, day care centers, nursery schools, playgroups, prekindergartens, basic schools, kindergartens, or infant, primary, and elementary schools. Whatever the settings are called, they serve the developmental and educational needs of children between the ages of four and eight years, give or take a year either side.

Project Work

In some countries, project work is referred to as theme or topic work. Others refer to a project as a unit. Some teachers combine project work with a learning-center approach. Although the meanings of these terms vary somewhat, they all emphasize the part of the curriculum that encourages children to apply their emerging skills in informal, open-ended activities that are intended to improve their understandings of the world they live in.

Terminology

Writing for a diverse readership requires difficult compromises with respect to terminology. For example, the term *early childhood education* is not as commonly used in Britain as in other English-speaking countries. In several parts of North America, the term may encompass children from birth to six, three to six, birth to eight, or four to eight years. In Britain the age span we address is usually referred to as the *early years*. Furthermore, the term *infant education*, as used in Britain for five- to seven-year-olds, has completely different meaning in most of North America, where infancy refers to babies.

The term *preschool* covers different age groups within some countries, as well as among them. In Britain, children in preschools are often referred to as the *under fives*, or even *rising fives*. At the present time in Britain more four-year-olds are being included in regular infant or primary schools in so-called *reception classes*. Some English-speaking countries imply different ages by the term *kindergarten*: in some, *kindergarten* is a translation for day care centers serving children from three to six years of age; in others, it is a small school for children from four to six years. The category *school years* also encompasses different age groups around the world, depending on the age at which school attendance becomes compulsory.

In the hope of minimizing some of the confusion of terms characteristic of the field of early childhood education, we have chosen to refer to programs serving children four and five years of age as *preschool education*, and those for five to eight years as *the school years*, even though the two groups overlap in age.

English-speaking countries also use different terms for other aspects of education. In general, North Americans share terms, and others employ British terms. We have attempted to present our ideas and examples bilingually, so to speak. Where we were unable to find a term common to all readers, we have noted a distinctly British usage by inserting a (Br.) notation. We appreciate the patience and understanding in cases where we have failed to address all readers. Although there are differences among early childhood educators in various regions and countries, we assume that all share common concerns and challenges.

USES OF THE BOOK

This book is intended to be used in a number of ways, depending on the reader's background and experience. Readers who are new to the project approach may find it helpful to begin with chapter 3. There they will find illustrations of project work and gain an impression of what some of the activities look like. Readers who have had some experience with project work may be especially interested in the specific suggestions offered in chapters 4 through 9. Readers with extensive experience using the project approach may find the research and principles discussed in chapter 2 especially helpful for explaining the value and appropriateness of project work to colleagues, administrators, and parents.

We do not intend the book to be used as a curriculum plan. Our purpose is to provide an introduction to the principles and practices of the project approach. We suggest ways that it can be applied and present examples that readers can use as a point of departure in the light of their own teaching preferences and contexts.

We hope to hear from readers about their own experiences with the project approach in working with young children.

ACKNOWLEDGMENTS

We owe thanks to many, not the least of whom are our own children and our own teachers. We are grateful also to the many students who have challenged us to find ways to help them understand and learn to use the project approach. We acknowledge with gratitude the many other teachers in North America, Britain, and several other countries in whose classrooms we have observed the life of projects and who have taken time to talk with us and write to us about their work.

We wish to express special thanks to the children and teachers of Rowanfield School, Cheltenham, where one of us was able to work as a classroom teacher at a time when the main ideas for this book were being formed. The illustrations used for the cover are based on the work of children in Rowanfield School.

We appreciate the comments of our colleagues who took the time and trouble to read preliminary drafts of the book and make helpful suggestions. We are indebted to Angela Andrews and Helen Hocking for permission to adapt their project web and journal excerpts for use in Appendix 1, and to Fay Moore for use of materials in Appendix 10. We are especially grateful to our friend and colleague Wendy Dewhirst, who made her cottage in the Yorkshire Dales available to us for several weeks at a time. There, we were able to meet and work together without the normal pressures of our places of work.

We are deeply indebted to Sheila Ryan not only for her painstaking and careful editing, but for encouraging us to keep working to complete the manuscript. Without her support, completion of this book would have surely been long delayed. Thanks are due also to Jane Harbor for her help with typing and correcting the manuscript.

We acknowledge also with our deepest thanks the patience, understanding, encouragement, and support of our husbands, Boris and David.

Lilian G. Katz
Sylvia C. Chard

CHAPTER 1

Profile of the Project Approach

Let us begin with a quick look at project work in progress in an early childhood classroom:

Several children are collaborating on a painting depicting what they have learned about the driving mechanism of the school bus. Their teacher is helping them label the steering wheel, horn, gearshift, ignition, accelerator, hand brake, brake pedal, turn indicators, windshield wipers, and inside and outside rearview mirrors.

A second small group is working on felt-pen drawings of parts of the motor, indicating where oil and water are added. The children make a diagram showing how fuel flows from the gas tank to the motor and how the exhaust makes its way through the tailpipe. As they work, they correct each other and make suggestions about what goes where and what details to include.

A third small group is finishing a display of their paintings showing the different kinds of lights inside and outside the bus. The display notes which lights are for signals and warnings and which serve to light the way ahead as well as inside. Some lights are red, some amber, and some white; some flash on and off and some are just reflectors. Their work is accompanied by a lively exchange of information and opinion about what they have seen and how to picture it so that other children can see what they mean.

A fourth group has prepared a chart of the gauges and dials on the dashboard, giving a basic idea of the information each one yields. Two of the children used a rope to establish the width and length of the bus. They have displayed their rope on a counter in front of a sign the teacher helped them to write:

OUR BUS IS:
2 ROPES WIDE & 6 ROPES LONG IT HAS 6 WHEELS & 42 SEATS.

These children are explaining to a classmate how they measured the bus. Earlier that day they had described the data-gathering processes to the principal of their school.

Two children are completing a large illustration of the safety features on the bus: fire extinguisher, emergency doors and windows, an emergency exit sign, and a first-aid kit.

Six children are playing in and around a large model of the school bus constructed in the classroom. The heavy cardboard container painted in traditional school bus colors by the children includes the name of the school, license plates, and other writing copied from the real bus. A few rows of seats made of large blocks and small chairs, steering wheel, and a rearview mirror stimulate the spontaneous, animated role play that includes a bus driver, traffic officers, and noisy passengers.

Although this project involved the children in a detailed study of their school bus, the knowledge gained will never be assessed on a standardized achievement test. But the example illustrates the main thesis of this book: Including project work in an early childhood education curriculum promotes children's *intellectual development by engaging their minds.*

WHAT IS A PROJECT?

A project is an in-depth study of a particular topic that one or more children undertake. It consists of exploring a topic or theme such as "going to the hospital," "building a house," or "the bus that brings us to school." Work on a project should extend over a period of days or weeks, depending on the children's ages and the nature of the topic. Preschoolers might spend two or three weeks on a hospital project; older children might spend twice as long. Unlike spontaneous play, projects usually involve children in advanced planning and in various activities that require several days or weeks of sustained effort. A shorter, impromptu project might be stimulated by an unexpected event or visitor. A project involving a study of the neighborhood or the weather might be extended over several weeks, and still others might be completed within a week.

An individual, a group, or the whole class might undertake a project. Preschoolers are more likely to work on projects in small groups rather than as individuals or as a whole class. Older children might have leaders who take some responsibility for different aspects of the work to be done.

WHAT IS THE PROJECT APPROACH?

We use the term *project approach* for several reasons. First, it reflects our view that projects can be incorporated into the early childhood curriculum in a variety of ways, depending upon the preferences, commitments, and constraints of teachers and schools. In some cases, project work takes up a large proportion of the curriculum. In other cases, project work is offered just two afternoons a week. Some teachers integrate it into learning centers; still others, especially at the preschool level, devote most of the curriculum to it.

Second, project work as an *approach* to early childhood education refers to a way of teaching and learning, as well as to the content of what is taught and learned. This approach emphasizes the teacher's role in encouraging children to interact with people, objects, and the environment in ways that have personal meaning to them. As a way of learning, it emphasizes children's active participation in their own studies. The content or topic of a project is usually drawn from the world that is familiar to the children. Thus one might expect projects in a rural school to focus on animals and crops cultivated on the nearby land. Children in a fishing village might be engaged in projects about boats, fishing, and fisheries. In an urban area, children can undertake projects about types of buildings, construction sites, factories, traffic patterns, vehicles, and the workers involved.

WHAT ARE THE AIMS OF THE PROJECT APPROACH?

Our advocacy of the project approach is rooted in our own ideological commitments and values related to the aims of education. An overall aim of this approach is to cultivate the life of the young child's mind. In its fullest sense, the term *mind* includes not only knowledge and skills, but also emotional, moral, and aesthetic sensibilities.

An appropriate education for young children should address the full scope of their growing minds as they strive to make better sense of their experiences. It encourages them to pose questions, pursue puzzles, and increase their awareness of significant phenomena around them. From four to eight years of age, most children still respond eagerly to adults' suggestions, contribute readily to group efforts, and try out new skills enthusiastically. Project work provides opportunities for them to do so. We recommend that the project approach be incorporated into the early childhood curriculum in the service of five major aims outlined below.

Intellectual Goals and the Life of the Mind

In recent years early childhood educators in North America, Britain, and elsewhere have been under increasing pressure to emphasize academic goals in the curriculum for young children. The academic curriculum is typically organized in lock-step fashion so that all children pass through the same sequences, ideally at the same ages, preferably on the same days. The three R's that dominate an academic curriculum are also typically broken into sequences of discrete skills. The children are formally instructed in small or in large groups and practice the skills through separate subtasks in workbooks and on work sheets. Largely mindless, these activities usually mean little to the children. The content is often unrelated to the world in which they live and learn.

A curriculum oriented toward academic goals puts a high priority on the needs, demands, and constraints of the academy itself and on acquiring the narrow range of skills and dispositions required to function within it. In such a curriculum, the activities and content have more vertical than horizontal relevance. *Vertical relevance* refers to instruction that prepares the learner for the next level of instruction—a kind of education "for the next life." *Horizontal relevance* refers to learning that equips the learner to solve current problems within and outside the classroom or school.

Many parents and school officials believe that the alternative to an academically oriented curriculum is focused on socialization and play. Sometimes labeled the *traditional* nursery or kindergarten approach, this alternative curriculum offers children the opportunity and materials for spontaneous play and amusing games. While there are several variations on this so-called traditional approach, they share a strong emphasis on spontaneous play as the significant medium for learning.

Our position is that neither the academic nor the traditional approach is adequate for the education of young children, mainly because both fail to engage the young child's mind sufficiently. The opportunity for socialization and play can benefit all young children during the early years. And certainly many children as young as five years can profit from some kinds of academic work. But in our view a developmentally appropriate curriculum should focus mainly on *intellectual* goals. By this we mean that the children's minds should be engaged in ways that deepen their understanding of their own experiences and environment.

In principle, the younger the children, the more important it is that most of the activities provided for them engage their intellects. As children grow, they become better able to address routine and repetitive academic tasks because they can more easily comprehend the need for drill and practice to attain skill proficiency. Teachers throughout the early years tend to overestimate children academically but underestimate them intellectually.

The children described at the beginning of this chapter were involved in a detailed study of their school bus. They examined it inside and out and inspected many aspects of it closely. Their minds were engaged in finding out about the parts of the bus, their functions, and the safety measures. The children had the chance to learn that everyday things can be full of interesting features to be studied in detail.

A Disney-world decor seen in many early childhood classrooms seems to set a tone that undermines cultivating the life of the mind. Slick pictures of smiling animals indicate where the books are located and what the learning centers are for. Children sometimes wear brightly colored crowns marked "good listener" or "fantastik helper." Implying that amusement and enjoyment are lumped together with education, the decor treats children more like pets than like sensible (though inexperienced) people.

While enjoyment is a desirable goal for entertainment, it is not an appropriate aim of education. A major aim of education is to improve the learners' understanding of the world around them and to strengthen their dispositions to go on learning. When educational practices succeed in doing so, learners find their experiences enjoyable. But enjoyment is a side effect or by-product of being engaged in worthwhile activity, effort, and learning.

Balance of Activities

Project work should not replace all current early childhood practices, nor should it be the total curriculum in the early years. Rather, as a significant portion of an educational program, project work can stimulate emerging skills and help children to master them.

Project work should complement and enhance what young children learn from spontaneous play as well as from systematic instruction. For preschool children, project work lends coherence and continuity to their work together. It is that part of the curriculum that the teacher intentionally guides. In this sense, a project is the relatively structured part of the curriculum. However, because a project is emergent and negotiated rather than totally preplanned by the teacher, it provides the less structured, more informal part of the curriculum in the school years.

We realize that many teachers are under strong pressure from school authorities, teachers of older children, and many parents to emphasize academic instruction at the expense of the more spontaneous and creative aspects of the curriculum. Nevertheless, for most four-year-olds, formal instruction in academic skills cannot be justified on the basis of available evidence (Schweinhart, Weikart, & Larner, 1986a; Karnes, Schwedel, & Williams, 1983). As children grow, their capacity to benefit from formal academic work increases. From the age of about five years, many children can be profitably engaged in some formal instruction. In our view of children's learning and development, the knowledge and skills acquired by formal instruction are likely to be strengthened by being applied. This implies a curriculum balanced with the kind of project work described in the chapters that follow.

School as Life

Another aim related to the project approach is for adults and children to see that school is life. The children's school experiences are real, daily life experiences; they are not a withdrawal from life, which is resumed only outside the school. From the child's point of view, school experiences are not contrived and institutional. As elsewhere, life in school should make varying demands on concentration, effort, challenge, and involvement. Some time should be free from external pressures, some time assigned to demanding work, and some allocated to relaxation. Including project work allows variation in the kinds of demands and pressures children encounter.

Older children are likely to see school as a place where certain feelings and concerns do not belong. Young children, however, have not yet acquired such a perspective. On the contrary, it is developmentally characteristic of young children to respond in a relatively undifferentiated way to all of their experiences. The stream of daily life experiences does not occur in categories such as science and history. The content of experience is more like events and topics than discrete disciplines. Project work is designed to free children's minds from the constraints of subject boundaries. In principle, the younger the children, the more integrated the curriculum should be.

Community Ethos in the Class

A fourth related aim of education is for the children to experience the class as a community. Community ethos is created when all of the children are expected and encouraged to contribute to the life of the whole group, even though they may do so in different ways. Project work provides ample opportunity for a cooperative ethos to flourish.

The children who studied their school bus, for example, shared a set of experiences they all had in common. Studying the bus in small groups and sharing their findings strengthened their sense of belonging to a community of young scholars.

Teachers play a major role in supporting the children's developing sense of belonging to the group and contributing to group life. Throughout the book we refer to this important aspect of education.

Teaching as a Challenge

Another aim of the project approach is for teachers to see their work as challenging. We have worked with teachers in a wide variety of situations and under diverse conditions. Some teachers must cope with poor physical facilities and a short supply of learning materials. Still other teachers have very large classes, poor staff–child ratios, or mixed age groups. Many teachers have two different groups of children per day, and thus both groups must share the space and equipment in the classroom. Although these realities frequently present severe problems, we have tried to emphasize that they can often be seen as challenges. The two examples below may be helpful.

The teacher of a morning group of four-year-olds was reluctant to undertake project work because she was afraid that the morning and the afternoon groups using the same room would spoil each other's work. Once she saw this difficulty as a challenge, however, she used it as a teaching situation. The morning group dictated a message to her for the afternoon group, saying, "We are building a police station in our class. Have you got some ideas?" The afternoon teacher read the message to her group, solicited their replies, and wrote them down. In the morning, the teacher read the afternoon group's message to her children, and they discussed its contents. The children in the morning group were able to carry on their project, which the afternoon children regularly inspected and commented on without interfering. Both groups learned something about transmitting information to people who are not seen, and they gained some fresh understanding of the function and value of written communications.

The second example is that of a teacher who arrived at school one morning to find that workers had started to repair the roof of her temporary classroom building. Neither she nor the principal had been forewarned, and no alternative classroom was available at the time. After brief discussion with the principal about possible courses of action, she decided to stay in the classroom and organize a day-long study of the whole happening. Some of the children were scheduled in pairs to observe the workers' progress throughout the day; others were assigned to interview them. Some of the children made a scale model of the classroom, roof and all. Others drew the tools, learned their names, and painted pictures of various aspects of the work. One of the workers was invited to talk to the class about roof repairs. The children studied the tools, different layers of roofing felt, and the bitumen (Br.), which had to be heated to specific temperatures. By the end of the day and on into the next, the children created a wall display describing the event in rich detail.

In these two examples, creative and constructive solutions were found in response to potential problems. Each teacher saw the situation in a positive light as a challenge, rather than as a constraint on what she could accomplish. Creative solutions to the predicaments of teaching cannot always be found. However, the disposition to respond to problems as challenges is worth cultivating in ourselves as well as in the children. A curriculum that limits the teacher primarily to daily instructional lessons or to setting out the same toys and equipment day after day can quickly become dreary and devoid of intellectual challenge.

Why Adopt the Project Approach?

The practices included under the rubric *project approach* are not new to early childhood or elementary education (Van Ausdal, 1988). Stewart (1986) asserts that the idea of learning through projects originally gained popularity in the United States, where it was advocated by both Dewey and Kilpatrick (p. 118). It can also be seen in Isaac's (1966) descriptions of children's work in England in the 1920s. In more recent times the project approach most closely resembles the Bank Street approach developed over many years at the Bank Street College of Education in New York City (Zimilies, 1987).

The description of the school bus project will no doubt remind many readers of "open education," an approach to teaching and learning during the late 1960s and early 1970s. These practices were identified, described, and advocated in Great Britain in the document that came to be known as the "Plowden Report" (Plowden Committee, 1967; Department of Education and Science, 1978). British educators gave them various labels such as "integrated day," "integrated curriculum," and "informal education." Silberman (1970) points out that the "Plowden Report" strongly emphasized that learning "is likely to be more effective if it grows out of what interests the learner, rather than what interests the teacher." Furthermore, "To suggest that learning evolve from the child's interest is not to propose an abdication of adult authority, only a change in the way it is exercised" (p. 209).

According to Dearden (1984), a main feature of open education and the Plowden philosophy was project work much like the project described at the beginning of this chapter and in the chapters that follow.

The practices identified with Plowden in Britain and open education in North America resemble the goals and practices advocated by the progressive movement of the 1920s: active engagement in projects, firsthand direct experience with the environment, learning by doing, as well as spontaneous play (Greenberg, 1987).

The complex reasons for the decline of progressive education at the end of the 1930s and the open education movement in the United States in the middle 1970s cannot be taken up in any detail here. As often noted, educational philosophies and ideologies swing back and forth in pendulum fashion (e.g., Kliebard, 1985). From time to time a particular approach to early childhood education is enthusiastically embraced and implemented. Within a few years a countermovement emerges, resulting in overcorrections in the opposite direction, only to be followed some years later by overcorrections in reverse. It seems to be in the nature of education in general, and the field of early childhood education in particular, that opinions and ideologies concerning appropriate curricula and methods are argued with great heat and conviction by each generation of parents, educators, and politicians (Dearden, 1983; Katz, 1977).

Perhaps one reason the open education movement declined was that many teachers believed themselves to be in an either–or situation: they felt obliged to adopt either progressive–open or formal–traditional methods. Many believed they had to abandon all of their previous practices, but were not given sufficient support for embracing the new ones (Gross, Giacquinta, & Bernstein, 1975). Furthermore, pressures from parents to ensure their children's academic success, whether merely perceived or actual, intimidated many administrators and teachers into abandoning plans for more informal open methods.

Why, then, should the project approach be reintroduced at this time? First, as we argue in chapter 2, a large body of research on children's development and learning in the last twenty years supports the proposition that the project approach is an appropriate way to stimulate and enhance children's intellectual and social development. Second, no evidence suggests that the project approach puts children's intellectual or academic development at risk. Third, the approach we propose is part of a balanced curriculum. During the preschool period a large part—but not all—of the curriculum is allocated to spontaneous play.

As children get older, increasing proportions of the curriculum are given to systematic instruction. It is our view that project work is an appropriate part of the curriculum throughout the preschool and elementary school years.

HOW DOES PROJECT WORK COMPLEMENT OTHER PARTS OF THE CURRICULUM?

We do not intend to urge teachers to discard all of their current practices and replace them with project work. We do recommend, however, that teachers experiment with project work in their present curriculum and adapt it to their own aims, philosophies, and contexts. Project work can thus complement and enhance what children learn through other parts of their curriculum.

In preschool settings, projects are among many other available activities. Appropriate materials and opportunities for spontaneous indoor and outdoor play, story reading, music, and other features of the typical preschool curriculum continue alongside project work. The work of a project differs from the other parts of the curriculum in that it is based on the plans and intentions of individuals or groups, typically in consultation with the teacher. Preschool activities such as block-building, water play, and spontaneous dramatic play are usually unrelated activities that do not focus on a topic or involve detailed advance planning or sustained effort over a period of days or weeks.

At the school-age level, however, project work is undertaken alongside systematic instruction. Bear in mind the underlying principle of the project approach: Skills applied to meaningful activities are more likely to be mastered (Department of Education and Science, 1978). For young children, workbooks and drill sheets are not purposeful enough for applying skills. Not only do such learning aids usually fail to engage children's minds, but they may also prevent children from understanding the purpose and use of a skill. Once children have reached school age, however, project work becomes a complement to systematic instruction.

Systematic instruction is an approach to teaching *individual* children a progression of interrelated subskills, each of which contributes to greater total proficiency in skills such as reading and writing. Systematic instruction refers to those skills that require specific and sequential subskills to attain proficiency. While some children can acquire these skills without systematic assistance, most profit from it. Furthermore, strengthening the disposition to apply the skills requires the provision of contexts in which their application is functional and

Table 1.   Four Distinctions Between Systematic Instruction and Project Work

Systematic instruction: *Skills acquisition* Extrinsic motivation	Project work: *Skills application* Intrinsic motivation
Child's willingness to work for the teacher and rewards is source of motivation.	Child's interest and involvement promote effort and motivation.
Teacher selects learning activities and provides materials at appropriate instructional level.	Child chooses from a variety of activities provided by the teacher; seeks appropriate level of challenge.
Teacher is the expert; sees the child as deficient.	Child is the expert; teacher capitalizes on child's proficiencies.
Teacher is accountable for learning and achievement.	Child shares accountability with teacher for learning and achievement.

purposeful. As used here, the term *systematic instruction* should not be confused with the popular American term *direct instruction* (Rosenshine, 1983), which refers to teaching the same subskills to a whole class or to children grouped by ability.

Formal systematic instruction in basic academic skills is not typically undertaken during the preschool years. Project work therefore does not differ as much from other aspects of the curriculum as it does in the school years. Both spontaneous play and project work are informal in organization. In the school years, however, systematic instruction is clearly formal, and project work clearly informal.

The nature and functions of project work in the school years can be better understood by examining how it is distinct from systematic instruction, yet complementary to it. At least four fundamental contrasts between the two approaches can be distinguished. As discussed below and summarized in Table 1, these contrasts indicate how project work can strengthen children's dispositions to use the skills acquired through systematic instruction.

Extrinsic and Intrinsic Motivation

Let us look first at the nature of children's motivation. Because acquiring basic skills is so important, some teachers may capitalize on the child's willingness to work for extrinsic rewards. This is especially true when a child's attention and persistence are difficult to secure by other means. By contrast, project work relies on intrinsic motivation. It capitalizes on the child's own interest in the work and on the appeal of the activities themselves. The learning is more diffuse than in formal instruction and involves a much wider range of possible activities. Because project work provides many options, children are rarely required to undertake one particular task rather than another. The information and activities vary widely in difficulty.

When children are intrinsically motivated, they respond in ways that encourage their disposition to work independently of the teacher, for example by helping one another. They can determine for themselves what they want to find out from books, reference materials, adults at home, and other children. By experimenting, children can determine the most appropriate methods of inquiry and sources of information. The sense of purpose with which children engage in a project activity is just as important as any product. The dispositions to exert effort, to strive for mastery in the face of difficulties, and to seek challenge, as described by Dweck (1986), can be strengthened when project work is regularly available.

Both extrinsic and intrinsic motivational processes are probably required for optimum participation in schooling, as well as in the larger world. In the school years, including both systematic instruction and project work means that the curriculum attends to the development of both types of motivation in a complementary fashion.

Teacher and Child Selection

In systematic instruction, the teacher selects the work and specifies the level at which it is to be carried out. In project work, the child makes these choices.

Rarely can the acquisition of complex skills, such as reading, wait until children spontaneously choose tasks for which learning to read is necessary. In systematic instruction for skill acquisition, the question of task difficulty is an important one. At least three levels of text readability have been proposed (Harrison, 1980). The first is called the "frustration level" when the reading material is too difficult for the child to benefit from it. The second is called the "independent level" when the material can be read independently but is not helping the child learn new skills. The third is the "instructional level" when the readability of the material optimizes the effects of instruction for a child. Such material is at an optimum level for acquiring the subskills needed to take the next steps towards full proficiency (Brown & Campione, 1984). Normally the teacher is considered responsible for continuously assessing and diagnosing the level at which the child is reading so that effective instruction can be given. Thus the teaching of complex academic skills usually requires teacher selection of tasks.

In applying skills in project work, however, the children are not required to progress through any recognizable sequence of stages. The children can safely choose their work from a range of options provided by the teacher. At times they may choose to tackle challenging problems, and at other times easy ones. The difference between selecting one level or the other may be accounted for by differences in background knowledge and interest in the project rather than by differences in ability level. Thus the two approaches are complementary: the teacher selects ability level that aids in acquiring skills, and the children select work that stimulates applying those skills.

Furthermore, the wide variety of project tasks and activities typically provides a context in which children can manifest their dispositions to seek appropriate levels of challenge. Note, however, that children should not feel compelled to work at the upper limits of their ability all of the time. A sufficient variety of activities and tasks should be available so that some can be done routinely, some in a free-wheeling fashion, and others to stimulate new learning. Lacking an optimum mix of these levels of task difficulty, many children will experience excessive stress and discouragement or may become bored by school.

Teacher and Child Expertise

Location of expertise is another distinction between systematic instruction and project work. In the formal teaching of reading, for example, the teacher is the expert responsible for instruction according to her diagnosis of the child's level of proficiency. The teacher directs and monitors skills practice, often through a sequence of graded workbooks, assignment cards, or work sheets. The teacher is the expert on the skills being taught.

In project work, children are encouraged to assess their own proficiency in applying skills, to monitor their own activity, and to select manageable tasks for themselves. Children become experts on their own learning. The teacher makes suggestions, but the children may be allowed to turn them down and judge for themselves. Poor judgment can be an occasion for teaching. For example, teacher and child can discuss ways of minimizing errors in the future. But if some errors pass unnoticed, they are not critical to the next stage of proficiency, as might be the case in progressing through a finely graded sequence of academic tasks.

A related distinction between systematic instruction and project work is based on alternative views of the learner. In formal academic work, children are seen as deficient in a skill and lacking a capability that they need. In project work, children are seen as already having proficiencies and capabilities and should be encouraged to apply them in meaningful contexts. Tasks used in systematic instruction are often taken out of context and have little personal meaning to the children. In contrast, the tasks in project work are undertaken in a context that makes sense to the children—what Donaldson (1978) calls "human sense." Because the context has personal meaning to the children, they can actively apply skills already developed, including observing, exploring, playing, investigating, reading, recording, discussing, and evaluating their own progress and the outcomes of their efforts.

By way of example, a teacher was helping a seven-year-old child who had difficulty with mathematics. In talking with the child, she discovered that he had a great interest in playing marbles. The playground culture of the school at that time included versions of the marbles game with a considerable range of quantitative information built into it. Pursuing this interest, the teacher asked the boy to show her his marbles and tell her about their different values in the game. She took two or three marbles in each hand and asked him which handful he would rather have. He immediately pointed out which one. She changed the combination and showed it to him for a split second. Again, he immediately indicated which of the two was more valuable. She increased the number of marbles and varied them to include more complex value combinations. By this means she discovered that the child's behavioral knowledge of number values was far ahead of any ability he had shown in the pencil-and-paper tasks of the mathematics curriculum. She then helped the child represent in written form his behavioral understanding of number values of the marbles. The exercise greatly facilitated his subsequent understanding of the pencil-and-paper tasks. Thus the teacher used the child's proficiency with numbers in a restricted context to teach him how to apply it more flexibly in other contexts. This incident clearly illustrates a point that French (1985) made:

> Perhaps cognitive development can be best characterized as a process of "gradual decontextualization." This position holds that cognitive skills first emerge and are practiced in specific contexts that demand their use, and that over time they may be generalized and extended beyond the initial context to be applied more flexibly. (p. 188)

Thus, when activities in a class include both systematic instruction and project work, teachers can use their expertise as required, and children can select the level of difficulty with which they are comfortable. These two kinds of learning can occur in complementary fashion. The principle is that, while adults know more about almost everything than young children do, children know what they understand and what it feels like to be themselves. In this sense, children are experts on their own learning needs. It is this expertise that the teacher must learn from in order to offer the most appropriate help. Children's own knowledge and experience also contribute to the development of a project. The teacher ensures an appropriate balance between systematic instruction and project work because the expertise of both teacher and children contributes to learning in complementary ways.

Teacher and Child Accountability

Now let us consider who is accountable for a child's accomplishments. In the case of teaching basic academic skills, teachers are maximally accountable. Their accountability is important precisely because they have the expertise and specialized resources available for helping children with learning difficulties. The teacher must make every effort to help any child experiencing difficulties acquiring academic skills.

In project work, however, the child and the teacher can be held accountable together. The cultivation of children's dispositions to reflect on and evaluate their own contributions to a project and to be accountable for them is an important feature of the project approach. If a child does not become proficient at drawing, for example, but does show a vivid imagination in creative writing, the parents and teacher are not likely to be greatly concerned. It is generally accepted that children vary in their strengths and limitations and have uneven patterns of achievement across all curriculum areas.

When the curriculum includes both systematic instruction and project work, the accountability for learning is shared by both teacher and children.

SUMMARY

During the preschool years, spontaneous play and project work are closely intertwined and occur side by side. Preschool children are encouraged to engage in spontaneous play related to the events and constructions they have worked on. For older children, each aspect of the curriculum—systematic instruction and project work—makes essential and complementary contributions to their education.

We write at a time when early childhood educators and other teachers through their associations and societies are urged on by various national reports to strive actively for professional status. One of the criteria of professional practice is that it is consistent with specialized knowledge based on the best available relevant research. The recent research that serves as a rationale for advocating the project approach is taken up in the chapter that follows.

Chapter 2

Research and Principles of Practice

In this chapter we will make the case that the project approach can bring curriculum and teaching practices closer to our current knowledge about children's development and learning. We present a rationale for including project work in early childhood education, a rationale based largely on insights from recent research findings. After discussing the concept of development, we present research and principles of practice relevant to four main kinds of learning. This section is followed by a brief discussion of the implications of research on topics related to the project approach.

THE CONCEPT OF DEVELOPMENT

Early childhood education has traditionally drawn heavily upon studies of human development. As academic specialties, child study and child development have contributed greatly to the field (Greenberg, 1987). The study of child development in particular is typically a major component of early childhood teacher preparation.

We find it helpful to think of the concept of development as having two major dimensions: the *normative* and the *dynamic* (Maccoby, 1984; Radke-Yarrow, 1987). Each of these dimensions has its own implications for education.

Normative Dimension of Development

As most commonly used, the concept of development draws on the normative dimension. This dimension addresses matters such as what most children can and cannot do at a given age or stage, for example,

17

what is typical and what is most frequently observed in children at two and three and five and nine years of age. We apply the normative dimension when we discuss how many words most children know at a particular age and the average age at which they can be expected to take their first step, to understand time, to conserve volume, and so forth. When we say that an activity is developmentally appropriate, speak of grade level achievement, or apply Gesell-type developmental measures, we are employing the normative dimension of the concept of development.

Dynamic Dimension of Development

The other major dimension is the dynamic one. This has three interrelated aspects. One deals with the ways that human beings *change* over time and with experience. It addresses the sequence of learning, the transformation that occurs in capabilities from one age to another, and the order in which the stages of development and learning occur. Thus some specialists study the sequential transitions in the stages of going from babbling babyhood to becoming a competent speaker of a language by age four or five.

A second aspect of the dynamic dimension is that of *delayed impact* (Radke-Yarrow, 1987). This concerns the way that early experience may affect later functioning, particularly with respect to affective and personality development. It attends to determinants of behavior that may be unconscious and due to early experiences no longer easily accessible to conscious attention. For example, early separation from mother may have a delayed impact on later mental health (Belsky, in press).

A third aspect of the dynamic dimension is the long-term *cumulative effect* of repeated or frequent experiences. An experience might have a benign effect on a child's development if it occurs only once in a while, but a harmful effect if it occurs frequently over a long period of time. A teacher might not worry if a child is occasionally confused by the directions for completing school tasks, but frequent confusion may have strong cumulative effects on the child's self-confidence. Occasional exposure to horror movies might not affect a child, but frequent exposure might have deleterious effects in the long term.

These three aspects of the dynamic dimension—change, delayed impact, cumulative effect—remind us to consider children's early experiences in light of their potential long-term consequences.

When both the normative and dynamic dimensions of development are taken into account, it seems reasonable to suggest that just because children *can* do something when they are young does not mean that they *should* do it. The distinction between what young children can do and what they should do is especially serious because most children appear willing, if not eager, to do what is asked of them. They rarely appear to be suffering, and some even enjoy the activities offered. Most young children are eager to please their teachers. But children's willingness and enjoyment are misleading criteria for judging the value of an activity. After all, young children enjoy junk food and poor television programs. Enjoyable experiences that people generally agree are not in a child's best interests can be tolerated on a few occasions. Their potentially damaging *cumulative effects* is what concerns many adults.

Within and across cultures it is well established that young children can engage in a wide variety of behavior. In some parts of the world, a large proportion assume heavy responsibility for the care of their younger siblings. Some toddlers are taught to "read" flash cards. Preschool children can perform rote counting up to the hundreds. Many young children fill out work sheets. They frequently work assiduously to receive tangible rewards such as gold stars and colorful stickers. But just because they can do so, does not necessarily imply that they should.

The concept of development can be seen in a preschool context in the following example of a small group of four-year-olds engaged in the "calendar ritual." With the children seated on the floor facing a large calendar showing the month of February, the teacher asks them what day it is. They call out days of the week in what appears to be random fashion, and by chance none offers the correct answer, which is Thursday. The teacher then asks, "What day was it yesterday?" The same array of guesses is offered, which fortunately includes Wednesday. She responds, "That's right! So what day is it today?" Eventually she coaxes them into agreeing on the correct answer.

When she asks next for the date (the 19th), no one replies. She then asks one of the children to come forward and write the correct numbers in the appropriate empty box on the calendar. When he hesitates, she suggests that he look at the number for yesterday. Unfortunately he looks in the box above rather than to the left of the empty one. Because it contains the number 12, the child says 13. Pointing out that he has looked "the wrong way," the teacher asks, "What comes after 18?" She thereby persuades him to agree on the date, which he manages to write almost legibly in the box. The teacher continues the exercise, soliciting the name of the month and the year.

This ritual consumed twelve to fifteen minutes. Apparently it had taken up about the same amount of time daily since the beginning of the school year. According to *normative* data on children's understanding of time (J. Blyth, 1984), the group observed in the calendar ritual probably understood little or nothing of the concepts involved in the calendar. If they had been asked what day or date it would be after dinner, very likely they would have been unsure of the correct answer. Daily discussions of the calendar seem appropriate for children a few years older than those observed. But four-year-olds lack the readiness to grasp the basic concepts of the calendar. Nevertheless, because the children were eager to please the teacher, they behaved as if they understood the concepts, when in fact they did not. The fact that children at age four can and do willingly engage in such an exercise does not justify including it their education.

While experience with this ritual is unlikely to be harmful if it occurs perhaps once a month, its potential long-term or cumulative effects warrant the concern of educators. Specifically, behaving occasionally as if one understands something when one really does not may not matter in the long run. But to do so daily over a long period of time—perhaps several months or longer—may have the cumulative effect of undermining children's confidence in their own questions, puzzles, doubts, and ultimately their own intellects. Such a cumulative effect seems antithetical to the purpose of education.

Children are always learning, but learning is a neutral term: children learn undesirable as well as desirable things, for example, to mistrust as well as to trust, to hurt as well as to help. The developmental question is not so much what children can do, or even how they learn. The critical developmental question for educators is what young children should do that best serves their development in the *long term*. Thus professional judgment about what young children should be doing takes into account not only what they can and cannot do at given ages, that is, the normative dimension of development, but also the best available knowledge of the long-term dynamic and cumulative effects of the choices at hand. The long-term developmental considerations can be applied to all of the important types of learning that continue throughout the early years of life.

FOUR CATEGORIES OF LEARNING GOALS

For discussion purposes, we find it helpful to categorize learning goals into four major types: knowledge, skills, dispositions, and feelings, all of which overlap in many ways. *Knowledge* refers to such things as schemata, ideas, facts, concepts, information, stories, and myths. *Skills* are discrete units of action that can be fairly easily observed and that are executed within a relatively short time. Examples of skills are recognizing the sounds of initial letters of words, drawing, and cutting with scissors. *Dispositions* can be roughly defined as habits of mind or tendencies to respond to situations in characteristic ways. Examples are inquisitiveness or persistence at a task in the face of difficulty. *Feelings* are subjective emotional or affective states such as feeling accepted, confident, or anxious.

Research relevant to each of these four categories of learning goals is discussed below, along with the principles of practice that the research implies.

Acquisition of Knowledge

Designing a curriculum for young children includes deciding what knowledge they should acquire. One basis upon which to make decisions is what the adults in the children's culture believe is important for them to know (Spodek, 1987). Another basis is our understanding of how children's knowledge develops and what they can understand as development proceeds.

Knowledge can be roughly defined as the "contents of mind" such as ideas, facts, concepts, constructs, and schemata. As children get older, knowledge becomes organized taxonomically and more hierarchically and is stored in memory in complex ways. Contemporary insights into the nature of development and learning in the early years reaffirm the idea that young children are intensely engaged in the quest for understanding their experiences (see Donaldson, 1983). Although investigators use various terms for the processes involved, they generally agree that the disposition to make sense of experience is powerful in the young child (W. A. L. Blyth, 1984).

The strength of this disposition was evident when Hughes and Grieve (1983) asked young children bizarre questions such as "Is milk bigger than water?" and "Is red heavier than yellow?" Five-year-olds attempted to treat these questions sensibly and to produce plausible answers: "Milk is bigger because it's got a color" and "Red is heavier than yellow because there's water in it" (pp. 108–109). Older, more knowledgeable and experienced children were much more likely to respond by pointing out that these were silly questions.

Most teachers of young children have a store of anecdotes about the interesting and often charming ways that children have made their own sense of experiences beyond their interpretive capacities. Children's sense-making activities can be seen as efforts to achieve the best understanding they can with the intellectual capacities they possess at a given stage of development. This suggests that a major responsibility of parents and teachers is to help children make fuller, deeper, and more accurate sense of their experiences. While parents contribute informally and spontaneously to children's understanding, teachers are the adults in children's lives who undertake this role deliberately and intentionally (see Katz, 1984a).

Behavioral and representational knowledge. In mature learners, knowledge is often classified into two main types. One type, *behavioral knowledge*, is primarily practical or procedural in nature (Pinard, 1986; Shuell, 1986). It refers to the learner's knowledge of how to enact various procedures and roles and to perform skills. Knowing how to ride a tricycle or push oneself on a swing are examples of behavioral knowledge in young children.

In contrast, *representational knowledge* consists of mental representations of the concepts, ideas, facts, propositions, and schemata that are abstracted primarily from direct and indirect experience. While behavioral knowledge is also represented in memory, it is represented primarily as the behaviors associated with events or related actions rather than as concepts or abstract symbols. Although abstract representational knowledge consists of schemata that may include behaviors, it consists mostly of higher order conceptual schemata abstracted and constructed from experience. A young child may have the behavioral knowledge of riding a bicycle or pushing a swing, but is unlikely to have abstract representational knowledge of how either of the behaviors works.

Young children's knowledge is mainly behavioral and is strongly embedded in the context in which it was learned. Three-year-olds may possess the behavioral knowledge to navigate throughout the rooms of their own home and perhaps their immediate neighborhood. But they probably cannot represent this knowledge abstractly in the form of a sketch or map. Even their ability to instruct someone else on how to get from one room to another may not fully match the extent of their behavioral knowledge. Similarly, five-year-olds typically have behavioral knowledge to speak their mother tongue fluently. They do not need abstract representational knowledge in the form of the rules of syntax and grammar to express themselves clearly and to use the language correctly for their own purposes.

Presumably children have a representation of the appropriate behavior. However, the younger the children, the more their representations are abstracted from real-life behavioral contexts. This feature of young children's knowledge and learning suggests that in principle the younger the children, the more context-embedded the curriculum activities should be. As Carey (1986) points out, learners "gain understanding by relating what they are reading (or hearing) to what they know, and this requires active, constructive work," (p. 1123). According to Carey, this view of the processes of learning provides "the cogni-

tive rationale (as opposed to the motivational rationale) for making education relevant to the learners' experiences and concerns" (p. 1123; italics added).

Even though the two types of knowledge, behavioral and representational, surely interact with each other in the course of daily life, the typology is useful for thinking about young children's intellectual development. A rich store of experiences for building behavioral knowledge can provide a firm basis for acquiring abstract representational knowledge. Thus a child can represent the behavior involved in navigating her house if she first has full behavioral knowledge of it. The developmental sequence seems to be *from* behavioral *to* representational knowledge, although the two forms of knowledge increasingly interact with each other as the child grows.

Formal instruction emphasizes the transmission of abstract representational knowledge. In traditional educational institutions, little thought is given to what behavioral knowledge the learners have and how it might be related to what is taught. Much contemporary conventional schooling, characterized by Brice-Heath (1987) as the "transmission model" of education, assumes that learners can acquire representational knowledge and transform it into the appropriate behavior. This is the reverse of the direction suggested above. While this may be the case for children in the later school years, a relevant principle for the early years is that an appropriate curriculum first strengthens children's behavioral knowledge and then introduces them to abstract representations directly related to it.

Event and script knowledge. Along similar lines, Schank and Abelson (1975) assert that much of our knowledge is represented in a form that resemble scripts. A script specifies the actors, actions, and props used to implement the goals of the scripted event. The extensive research of Nelson and her colleagues (Nelson & Seidman, 1984; Nelson, 1986; French, 1985) on how young children's representations of knowledge develop from scripts provides useful insights for early childhood curriculum planning.

Nelson (1986) points out that "the young child's cognitive processing is contextualized in terms of everyday experience" (p. 4.) and that "real world knowledge comes to the child almost exclusively from direct experience . . . primarily from the analysis of [her] own experience rather than from mediated sources" (p. 5). Nelson suggests that children are constantly engaged in reorganizing the data they collect from experience, first into events and then into scripts.

An *event* representation is a memory of an event and all of the associations the child has with it. For example, the "bedtime" event would be represented in memory with the objects, persons, and other salient matters related to it.

A *script* representation is a memory of an event and its associations that includes temporal sequences of what the participants do and say to each other as the event unfolds. Scripts "involve people in purposeful activities, and acting on objects and interacting with each other to achieve some result" (Nelson, 1986, p. 11). Thus a young child can represent the sequence of events contained in her bedtime routines. At times young children can in fact become quite indignant if the sequence is changed by leaving out even a minor detail.

Scripts can have any number of subscripts. Bedtime scripts may include subscripts dealing with undressing, bathing, or story-reading. The script "going shopping" may have subscripts dealing with waiting at the bus stop and paying the fare or getting into the car, fastening the seat belt, and walking from the parking lot. As scripts become well learned, they function automatically and alleviate the need to wonder what behavior is appropriate in standard situations (e.g., in restaurants). The richer the background experiences of the accumulating scripts, the more processing and abstracting will be stimulated.

In the preschool years, scripts are organized around familiar sequences and the behavior and props involved in them. Observation of children during spontaneous play gives us a sample of the script knowledge they are building. Thus play is frequently about life at home, school, and other scenes and settings to which they have been exposed.

During the early years, children develop scripts that have two kinds of features. The first are the invariant features such as what *always* happens when they go shopping (selecting items, paying for them, carrying them home). The second are the *optional* features that are often, occasionally, or rarely included in the event (going shopping with mother, or with father, or with grandma). With age and experience, children develop scripts that become longer, more detailed and complex, and less bound by direct firsthand experience.

Young children, then, constantly assimilate information to the scripts they already know and accommodate their script representations to make sense of new experiences. As children share scripts with others in the course of spontaneous interaction and more formal discussion, scripts assume a public form: they include the same features as the scripts of other members of the culture. Children gradually recognize what is idiosyncratic within their own experience and what is held in common with others' experience. For example, the breakfast event has public, culturally shared elements. Within any culture, however, individuals may have breakfasts that take very different forms. As children work on projects, the teacher can capitalize on the pool of event knowledge in a class of children from diverse backgrounds.

Nelson (1986) suggests that, while older children and adults learn from indirect or secondary sources of knowledge, such as textbooks and formal instruction, young children are unable to do so. Indirect sources of knowledge are not easily available to them because they are "unable to make use of language to construct world knowledge independently of their own prior experience for several years after first learning to talk" (p. 5). Children can learn much from stories and books as long as they can relate the knowledge in them to their own direct experience.

The research on script knowledge suggests that the curriculum in the early years should include opportunities for children to explore and act out familiar events and to exchange with each other and with adults the information they have about those events. In principle, then, the younger the children, the more the content of their activities should be event based; also, more opportunities should be provided for acting out scripts.

The variety of backgrounds that children bring to the group enriches the sources of information about how different people enact familiar events and what they do often, only occasionally, or rarely in relation to common scripts. Projects involving familiar events can be used to introduce new variations and information related to them. Project work on topics familiar to the children can provide contexts in which they can refine and add to their growing repertoire of scripts.

Acquisition of Skills

Skills are small units of action that can be fairly easily observed or inferred from observable behavior. The accumulation of a repertoire of skills continues to be a common basis for designing curricula for young children (Schwartz & Robison, 1982). The list of skills that young children learn spontaneously or with the help of adults is very long. It includes many kinds of physical, social, communicative, and cognitive skills of varied specificity. Teachers typically use systematic procedures to help children acquire basic skills, especially those related to reading, mathematics, and writing. While many children may be able to acquire such skills spontaneously, most need someone else to help master them.

Virtually all learners require an optimum amount of practice to achieve proficiency with skills. Practice can take the form of drill and exercises. But practice also occurs during activities to which the skills are applied. Including project work in the early childhood curriculum provides opportunities for the acquisition *and* practice *and* application of many skills. Almost all projects of interest to young children provide contexts for acquiring and applying emerging skills in literacy, numeracy, and problem solving.

Social competence. Even though strongly linked to social knowledge (French, 1985), social competence is discussed here primarily in terms of the social skills developed during the early years. Although definitions of social competence vary, they generally include the capacity to initiate, develop, and maintain satisfying relationships with others, especially peers. Social competence includes turn-taking and negotiating skills, approach strategies, and a wide variety of communication skills.

The criterion of social competence does not require that all children be social butterflies. It is not a source of concern if a child chooses to work or play alone, as long as he or she is capable of interacting productively and successfully with another when social interaction is desired, appropriate, or necessary.

Recent evidence is persuasive that young children who fail to develop minimal social competence during the first five or six years are at significant risk in adulthood (Asher, Renshaw, & Hymel, 1982; Gottman, 1983). Among the risks are a greater probability of becoming a school dropout and a delinquent (Parker & Asher, 1987) and of experiencing problems related to mental health and marital adjustment.

Achieving social competence involves many complex processes beginning in early infancy. It should be noted that both appropriate and inappropriate social responses are learned through interaction with peers. Maladaptive patterns of social responses may be intensified and strengthened during interaction unless the child is helped to alter them. Simply providing group interaction does not guarantee that all young children will acquire desirable peer interactive skills. Many children need adult help to master them.

In the preschool period, inadequate social skills are unlikely to be improved through formal instruction. Rather, they may be modified if a knowledgeable teacher intervenes in the course of a child's interaction with peers. Fortunately, teachers now have a range of techniques available for fostering the development of social competence (Burton, 1987; Katz, 1984b).

We have no reason to assume that the development of the neurological system limits a child's capacity to acquire new social competence after age five or six. Rather, the long-term cumulative effects of social difficulties in early childhood may be accounted for by a *recursive cycle* phenomenon. According to the principle of the recursive cycle, once an individual has a given behavior pattern, reactions to him or her tend to elicit more of that behavior or characteristic. For example, children who are likable, attractive, and friendly tend to elicit positive responses in others fairly easily. Because they receive such positive responses, they become more likable, attractive, and friendly, and a positive cycle continues.

Similarly, children who are unattractive, unfriendly, and difficult to approach or enjoy tend to be avoided or rejected by others. In response to this avoidance and rejection, they tend to repeat the patterns that make them even more unattractive, often with increased intensity. This sequence increases the likelihood that they will be avoided or rejected more often; thus a debilitating cycle becomes well established. This general principle can be applied to many kinds of behavior and learning, but especially to social behavior (see also Patterson, 1986).

Once children are launched into a positive cycle of social interaction, they have increasing opportunties to acquire new social competence and to refine skills already in their repertoire. However, opportunities to learn new social skills gradually diminish for the child caught in a negative recursive cycle. Poor patterns of social response, followed by increasing rejection or neglect by others, result in fewer opportunities to learn new, improved patterns. Unfortunately, a young child cannot break a negative cycle alone. Even for adults, breaking dysfunctional patterns of social responses by oneself is very difficult. The young child's capacity to understand the cause of his or her social difficulties and the needed adjustments is virtually nil. Adults must intervene to launch a child into a positive cycle.

The principle of the recursive cycle implies that young children should be engaged in interactive processes, especially in the company of teachers who have special skills for helping children maximize the educative potential of peer interaction. For young children, social competence cannot usually be acquired from direct instruction. But teachers can help them by suggesting and teaching them effective social strategies during on-going, purposeful, social interaction.

Given the plasticity of young children, if we respond to their need for developing social competence during the early years, we can help them enter a positive cycle and ease the anguish of social difficulties in childhood. If intervention is postponed until middle childhood or early adolescence, substantial resources from a mental health agency may be required. Even so, intervention may be too late to help change the negative cycle. The persistence of social difficulties is not caused by a critical period in the growth of the central nervous system, but by the stability of patterns of social response that children cannot change by themselves. The younger the child, the easier it is to break a negative recursive cycle.

For some children, problems with schoolwork stem from social difficulties. For other children, problems with social interaction stem from difficulties with their schoolwork. In either case, recent research on children's social competence suggests that teachers' concern with the social development of young children is well founded and should be given as much weight in planning and teaching as is given to children's physical and intellectual development (Asher et al., 1982). Social competence can be strengthened when children engage in purposeful and worthwhile activities together. Because project work typically includes social interaction, teachers have many opportunities to help strengthen young children's emerging social competence.

Communicative competence. Virtually everyone concerned with young children's learning recognizes that early childhood is a critical period in the development of communicative competence. Communicative competence includes complex knowledge as well as skills. Contemporary research indicates that all three basic functions of language, namely, communication, expression, and reasoning, are enhanced when children engage in conversation (Nelson, 1985; Wells, 1983, 1986). Passive exposure to language is not enough by itself to enhance communicative competence.

Children in the early years are not yet expert conversationalists. Most teachers recognize the difficulty of encouraging conversation during group sessions. Much effort is given to reminding children that their turn to speak has not yet come. A kindergarten teacher was observed attempting to engage a whole class of five-year-old children in group discussion by asking each in turn, "What is your news today?" Each child struggled to find something headline-worthy to report to his or her uninterested, squirming companions. Perhaps some of these children were learning to "listen" as the teacher intended, but many appeared to be learning to "tune out" their stammering classmates.

Conversations are a special type of interaction in which the content of each participant's contribution is contingent upon the other's in a sequential string of responses. If the contributions are not sequentially contingent, the interaction consists of parallel monologues. The work of Bruner (1980) and others suggests that conversations are most likely to occur when children are in small groups of three or four, with or without an adult present. Furthermore, it is reasonably clear that children are most likely to converse when something interesting enough to them occurs in context (Bruner, 1980; Clark & Wade, 1983). Findings of the Oxford Research Project indicate that the content of interactions in preschool programs is typically managerial and fails to engage the kind of interest that would support genuine conversations among the children.

Blank (1985) also suggests that conversations are more likely to be prolonged when adults make comments to children rather than ask questions. Many teachers attempt to engage children in conversation by asking them questions. There are, however, several types of questions, not all of them equally likely to result in sustained conversation (Wood & Wood, 1983). The most common type of questioning that teachers use is *interrogation*. Questions like "What color is your shirt?" or "What did I say?" are examples of interrogations, questions whose answers the adult already knows. Interrogatory questions have a distinctly unreal aspect to them. A nursery teacher was observed questioning her pupils about a visit they had made to an aquarium the day before. She asked the children, "How did the fish get into the tank?" One of them responded earnestly by asking her, "Have you forgotten already?"

One effect of the excessive use of interrogations is to create interactive patterns that are phony and unlike discourse outside of school. Another is to make respondents feel intimidated or even threatened. When interrogatory questions dominate interaction in the class, pupils often become reluctant to reveal their confusion and to ask for help.

An alternative approach is for the teacher to ask children *soliciting* questions, which encourage them to give her information she does not already have. She can ask, for example, "Is that color shirt one of your favorites?" "Do you especially like the color blue?" The child's answer can then be responded to with appropriate comments and conversation. Occasionally an interrogatory question is appropriate, however. If so, the teacher could say, "I want to know if you know your address. Tell me what it is." In this way, the teacher's question is genuine, and her relationship to the child remains authentic.

A principle suggested by much recent research is that young children's commmunicative competence can be enhanced by work in small groups on projects that provide rich content for conversation. Another principle is that children's conversational interactions are facilitated when the teacher offers comments and solicits their opinions and ideas.

Academic skills. Curriculum approaches employed in early childhood programs vary in the extent to which they emphasize the teaching of basic academic skills (Evans, 1975; Maccoby & Zellner, 1970; Schweinhart et al., 1986a). Some approaches achieve a more even balance than others do between the proportion of time allocated to basic skills instruction and spontaneous play. In general, including instruction and exercises in basic skills for four- and five-year-olds has increased significantly in the last decade. This matter has been the subject of vigorous discussion and debate among educators and parents (Bereiter, 1986; Bredekamp, 1987; Gersten, 1986; Kamii, 1985; Schweinhart et al., 1986a, 1986b).

Many preschool children show a spontaneous interest in various aspects of literacy (Schickedanz, 1985). Certainly these interests should be encouraged and supported, albeit in an informal way. As indicated in chapters 4 and 5, project work provides many opportunities for children to apply the rudiments of basic skills they are developing.

Observation of children in a wide variety of academically oriented programs confirms the fact that young children *can* engage in structured exercises designed to instruct them in basic skills such as phonics, counting, and handwriting. But the extent to which they *should* do so must be evaluated in light of the potential cumulative effects that these exercises may have on the development of desirable dispositions.

Development of Dispositions

Broadly defined, dispositions are relatively enduring habits of mind and action, or tendencies to respond to categories of experience across classes of situations (Katz, 1985). We use the term *disposition* in very much the same way that Webb (1974) uses the phrase *attitude of mind* in her discussion of the concept of education (p. 56).

Buss and Craik (1983) define dispositions technically as "summaries of act frequencies." They assert that when an individual enacts certain behaviors with sufficient frequency, one can infer that he or she has a given disposition. In this sense, the term *disposition* denotes many of the same qualities as the term *personality trait* (Katz & Raths, 1985), and these qualities are manifested in a variety of behaviors that occur with relative frequency (Buss & Craik, 1983).

A disposition is not an "end state" similar to the mastery of a piece of knowledge or the command of a particular skill. Dispositions are habits of action and reaction to classes of events and situations. Desirable dispositions include curiosity, humor, generosity, and helpfulness. Undesirable dispositions include avarice, quarrelsomeness, and callousness.

Skills and dispositions. For at least two reasons, dispositions deserve the attention of teachers during the early years. The first and more obvious reason is that educators and parents readily nominate many dispositions when asked to indicate their hopes for the outcome of education. They generally agree on the desirability of encouraging children's curiosity, creativity, resourcefulness, independence, initiative, responsibility, and other positive dispositions.

The development of dispositions also deserves attention because some approaches to teaching knowledge and skills may possibly undermine the disposition to use them. Of particular concern is the risk that introducing formal academic or direct instruction in the early years may jeopardize the development of desirable dispositions. There is no compelling evidence that early introduction to academic work guarantees success in school in the long term. But there is reason to believe that, because of cumulative effects, early introduction could work against developing desirable dispositions and "attitudes of mind," as Webb calls them (1974, p. 56).

The main issue is that early achievements may threaten development of the dispositions to be readers and appliers of mathematical skills, given the amount of drill and practice usually required for success in applying these skills at an early age. This issue can be referred to as the *damaged disposition hypothesis* (Katz, 1985).

The risk of undermining desirable dispositions related to education may go unnoticed for two reasons. First, young children who are given formal direct instruction in basic skills appear to do well on the kinds of standardized tests used by school authorities. Second, dispositions (e.g., curiosity, interest, involvement) are rarely evaluated in early childhood programs. Furthermore, when a curriculum is designed as a strongly remedial program and allocates large proportions of time to practicing skills, the initial test results are generally encouraging, and the program can report positive results. But these positive outcomes are mainly of short duration. On the other hand, curriculum approaches that provide for strengthening dispositions such as interest, initiative, and curiosity by allowing for play and project activities show relatively unimpressive test results in the short term, but considerable benefits in the long term.

Thus the damaged disposition hypothesis seems to be a reasonable interpretation of the results of several longitudinal studies (Karnes et al., 1983; Miller & Bizzell, 1983; Schweinhart et al., 1986a; see also Walberg, 1984; Consortium for Longitudinal Studies, 1983). As we look at the results of these studies, the early pressure on young children to perform academic tasks taught by direct instruction (e.g., practice in phonics, workbook exercises) appears quite harmless or even beneficial at first. Many children *can* perform the tasks involved. But professional educators are obliged to take into account the potential cumulative effects of early experiences, no matter how benign they appear at the time they occur.

Results from longitudinal studies suggest that curriculum design for young children should be approached in a way that optimizes the simultaneous acquisition of knowledge, skills, *and* desirable dispositions. It is clearly not very useful to have skills if the disposition to use them is undermined in the process of acquiring them. On the other hand, having the disposition without the skills is also an unreasonable educational goal. The challenge, then, is to help the learner with both the acquisition of skills and with desirable dispositions that invoke the application of those skills.

Teachers can help by being alert to situations where it is advisable not to require further practice or more workbook exercises, lest a disposition to be a writer, for example, be weakened by excessive drill. This view of the relationship between skills and dispositions reflects the principle that emphasis on them must be balanced so that they are simultaneously enhanced. Identifying and observing children's dispositional development should thus be taken into account in teacher decision making.

Development of interest. One of the important dispositions of concern to educators of young children is *interest* or the capacity to "lose oneself" in an activity or concern outside of oneself. Although frequently used by educators, psychologists, and others, the term *interest* is difficult to define with precision. We use it to refer to the disposition to pursue an activity or goal in the absence of expected rewards. We include the tendency to become deeply absorbed enough in an activity to pursue it over an extended period of time, with sufficient commitment to accept its routine as well as novel aspects. Sometimes called "intrinsic motivation" (Deci & Ryan, 1985; Morgan, 1984), "continuing motivation" (Maehr, 1982), or "self-directed learning" (Benware & Deci, 1984), this disposition in rudimentary form appears to be present in the normal human at birth and to be affected by a variety of social–psychological processes throughout childhood.

Recent research indicates that children's interest and intrinsic motivation are affected by the kind of feedback they receive (Ryan, Connell, & Deci, 1985). Studies of the overjustification effect (Lepper, 1981) suggest that, when children are rewarded for tasks in which they had initially shown spontaneous interest, the reward is followed by diminished interest. In other words, rewards may reduce children's desire to engage in an activity spontaneously. The term *overjustification effect* reflects the idea that the satisfaction children derive from activities undertaken spontaneously provides its own justification. Offering a reward therefore "over" justifies the activity. The researchers suggest that children respond to such rewards by saying to themselves, as it were, "It must be wrong to like doing X if I am given a reward for doing it" (Deci & Ryan, 1982).

Hunter and Barker (1987) have analyzed the effects that rewards have on children's self-attributions about their own efforts. They point out that, when extrinsic rewards are made salient, children have no choice but to attribute their effort to a factor or force outside themselves. If, on the other hand, rewards are not obvious, children can attribute their effort to their own initiative and to forces inside themselves. Hunter's and Barker's analysis suggests that children are less able to perceive the responsibility for what happens to them as their own if extrinsic rewards are overemphasized in the classroom.

Similarly, in an experiment with preschoolers on ideational fluency (one index of creativity), Groves, Sawyers, and Morgan (1987) showed that children in the rewarded group scored lower than nonrewarded groups on creativity tasks, thus "supporting the growing body of evidence that rewards are detrimental to creative functioning." Boggiano and Main (1986) showed that the *bonus effect* of a reward can change the interest value of the activity for which the reward is given. Experiments on the bonus effect indicate that, when participation in one activity is contingent on having completed another, the latter's value is automatically depressed. Thus, if we were to insist that carrots can be eaten only if the dessert is finished (the reverse of the usual order), the desirability of carrots would increase substantially. The appeal of the dessert also becomes depressed. Needless to say, the bonus effect is bound to be restricted: increases in the liking for some foods are likely to be limited.

The deleterious effects of rewards and bonuses apply especially to activities that children originally find appealing. Special care must therefore be taken not to offer rewards for those activities. Since most young children are easily attracted to almost any novel activity, the practice of introducing tangible rewards is generally unwarranted.

The growing body of research on the effects of rewards and bonuses also implies that the tendency of teachers to tell children they may do art work only after completing their reading assignments is likely to depress the value and liking that children have for reading. They may perceive a message that little satisfaction can be expected from reading. Furthermore, making art activities contingent on completing other work may also give children mixed messages about the teacher's view of the value of art. It is unrealistic to expect children to be equally enthusiastic about all of the activities offered. Still, teaching strategies that unwittingly reinforce negative attitudes toward any of them should be avoided.

A parallel line of research on the development of interest suggests that when positive feedback is general in nature, productivity increases but interest declines (deCharms, 1983). Children are likely to respond to general positive feedback by increasing the amount of work they produce, but are likely to show less willingness to work on the tasks when the feedback is withdrawn. General positive feedback includes global comments such as "Very good!", "Well done!", "Great!" and the drawing of smiling faces or putting decorative stickers or gold stars on the children's products. When positive feedback is specific, however, particularly if it includes information about the competence of the work, children's willingness to continue without external pressure increases, although the amount of work produced does not increase. Specific, informative feedback is called a "tribute," and general, nonspecific feedback is called an "inducement." A tribute is associated with increasing interest in the task, whereas an inducement is associated with loss of interest but increased productivity except when rewards are withdrawn.

Along similar lines, Grolnick and Ryan (1987) compared the effects that different amounts of control, direction, and spontaneity have on children's motivation in experimental learning conditions. The researchers reported evidence of greater deterioration in rote recall several days following the experimental lesson that had greater control and direction. The finding "suggests that material learned under strong external pressures may be less likely to be maintained" (p. 897). The data also showed that under conditions in which the learners became apprehensive about grades, rote learning was promoted, but it "undermined interest and active integration of the material" (p. 897).

It is not yet clear how rewards and general positive feedback exert their negative effects on interest. But it seems reasonable to assume that they distract children from involvement in the tasks at hand. Mc-Cullers, Fabes, and Morgan (1987) examined the link between the detrimental effects of rewards on interest and subsequent immediate task performance. Their view is that "the adverse effects of material rewards are due to a temporary, reward-induced regression in psychological organization and function" (p. 1027). They assert that rewards shift subjects to a more "primitive" level of psychological functioning and have the effect of "changing the level of challenge from an optimal (intrinsically motivating) to a nonoptimal one" (p. 1032). Thus "tasks that are interesting and challenging under nonrewarded conditions become frustratingly difficult under reward [conditions]" (p. 1032). Mc-Cullers et al. suggest that when a reward is anticipated, it is reasonable to choose simpler, less challenging tasks by which to improve one's chances of obtaining the reward. Occasional striving for rewards and honors may be appropriate and beneficial. However, the cumulative effects of frequent and constant expectation of rewards from early childhood on may damage interest and challenge seeking in the long run.

Academically oriented programs typically emphasize general positive feedback, ostensibly to give children feelings of success and to spur productivity. This strategy appears to work well to induce young children to keep working at discrete, disembedded, decontextualized, and often very trivial tasks. Few of the kinds of tasks offered in such programs seem to engage children's inquisitive minds. Most young children approach these tasks quite willingly early in their school experience. However, the research on the effects of rewards strongly suggests that children may suffer academic "burn-out" after two or three years of general, positive, extrinsic rewards.

Curricula and teaching methods that attempt to provide children with constant amusement, fun, or excitement also risk undermining the development of children's disposition to be interested and absorbed in worthwhile activities (Katz, 1977b). For example, telling stories of the romanticized, unlawful activity of pirates is unnecessary to make the topic of the sea interesting. The size, force, and sound of the waves, the movement of the tides, the expanse of sandy beach, seaweed, pebbles and shells, soaring cliffs, teeming tide pools, and much more of the real world around the sea are sufficiently intriguing and engaging to children without extraneous inducement.

The teacher's role in strengthening children's dispositions to be interested in relevant and worthwhile phenomena is a complex and critical one. If dispositions are to be strengthened, opportunities to manifest them must be available. In the case of interest, the topics and activities themselves can be the source of satisfaction. Interest can also be strengthened when other people, particularly adults, acknowledge and appreciate its expression. For example, if a child asks a question while interacting with others, the teacher might return a day or two later with a pertinent artifact, indicating that she has recognized the child's expression of interest. She might say, "Yesterday you were wondering what hermit crabs look like. Well, I found a book with some pictures of them and thought it might interest you."

Interest and the capacity for absorption can be strengthened when children are encouraged to engage in projects that call for sustained effort and involvement over a period of several days or weeks. Such projects provide contexts for extending, elaborating, and continuing work and play (Rosenfield, Folger, & Adelman, 1980). Academic exercises and drills are usually presented to children as one-shot tasks to be completed within brief periods and rarely include extended or continuing involvement in a topic. Workbook exercises seldom evoke the disposition to make a second or third attempt at mastery. Typically each work sheet is handed in for correction and returned on a later day. The principle behind project work is that activities lasting an extended period of time strengthen the disposition to become involved and absorbed in mind-engaging work.

The disposition to lose oneself in an activity may be threatened by frequent interruptions. A classroom schedule that segments the day into activities lasting only fifteen or twenty minutes may undermine the disposition to become deeply involved in worthwhile effort. The daily program for young children should be flexible rather than fragmented in allocating time to various activities.

Effort, mastery, and challenge seeking. Extensive research by Dweck (1986, 1987) suggests that the goals teachers set have significant cumulative effects on children's dispositions toward effort, mastery, learning, persistence, and challenge seeking. Dweck asserts that school tasks can be set in terms of *performance* goals or *learning* goals. When a teacher introduces an activity by saying, "Today I want to see how good you are at X" or "How many problems you can get right" or "How well you can do," she sets performance goals. If, on the other hand, the teacher says, "Today I want to see how much you can learn" or "How much you can find out about X" or "I would like you to experiment and find out how far and how fast these cars roll on different surfaces," she sets learning goals.

These two conditions arouse different kinds of responses that affect children's dispositions toward effort and mastery. Under conditions of performance goals, children focus on gaining favorable judgments of their ability or avoiding negative ones. Under conditions of learning goals, children seek to increase their understanding or mastery of something new. Dweck (1986) defines the mastery disposition as adaptive, accompanied by "challenge seeking and high, effective persistence in the face of obstacles" (p. 1040). She defines the maladaptive disposition as helplessness, manifested by "challenge avoidance, low persistence in the face of difficulty" (p. 1042), accompanied by negative affect, anxiety, and negative self-attribution with respect to ability. The evidence also indicates that adaptive and maladaptive dispositions are independent of actual intellectual ability (Dweck & Leggett, 1988).

According to many studies, these two types of goals produce different effects on children's concerns as they address the tasks assigned. Under performance goals, children show concern about their ability. The confident ones may accept the task eagerly, though a few will worry lest they fail to measure up to their reputations as highly able on a particular occasion. Other children tend to engage in defensive withdrawal from the task to avoid expected negative judgments of their ability. Performance goals "promote defensive strategies that can interfere with challenge seeking" (Dweck, 1986, p. 1043). As Dweck's experiments revealed, children faced with learning goals chose challenging tasks regardless of whether they believed themselves to have high or low ability; they were also not unwilling to display their ignorance. Tending to think more about the required skills and the interest of the topic, they were less oriented internally toward their own ability and how they would look to others.

In lessons oriented toward performance goals, children who do not succeed tend to attribute their failure to their lack of ability. This kind of self-attribution usually leads to anxiety, which may interfere with their performance, and ultimately to withholding effort. A few children even become overwhelmed with worry about goal attainment. During learning-goal assignments, children perceive obstacles and difficulties as cues to increase their effort, to analyze and vary their strategies, and thus to improve their work. As Dweck (1968) points out, "The more children focus on learning or progress, the greater the likelihood of maintaining effective strategies (or improving their strategies) under difficulty or failure" (p. 1044).

The two types of task goals also give rise to different sources of satisfaction. Children perceive the performance-goal condition as an opportunity to display their abilities and take pride in them if indeed they are able, or they are embarrassed and ashamed when they fail. Children may come to the conclusion that effort indicates low ability. They may then attempt to disguise or deny that they have to apply real effort, fearing it will reveal that they have little ability. Children with a strong performance orientation derive satisfaction in outshining others and in the failure of others, and they enjoy a competitive reward structure.

In the case of learning goals, children enjoy the effort involved and the mastery achieved. Learning-oriented children have also been found to be more magnanimous toward their peers in noncompetitive situations (Dweck, 1986). Research also indicates a greater transfer of learning and more active attempts to apply what has been learned to novel problems.

According to one hypothesis about the possible outcome of extensive experience with performance goals, children who see themselves as having moderate or low ability come to disavow grades, test scores, and other indexes of performance. This hypothesis is related to Dweck's assertion (1987) that (in the United States at least) people acquire in the early years a strong cultural belief that ability is a fixed entity: one either has ability or not. Repeated pressures to perform would be accompanied by repeated exposures to one's own inadequacies. One way of coping with these exposures might be to distance oneself from the institution that passes judgment and from its workers, methods, and symbols.

The potentially negative effects of overemphasis on performance goals are similar to the detrimental effects of rewards. In an educational setting where teachers encourage working for rewards, children would be unwise or even foolish to undertake risky or challenging tasks. The most adaptive response is to do the simplest tasks to increase the chance of obtaining the rewards the adults put so much stock in. Although working for a reward might be appropriate or harmless on rare occasions, repeated daily injuctions to strive for rewards could have undesirable, cumulative effects in the long term. Contrary to common sense, "Continued success on personally easy tasks with a performance goal . . . is ineffective in producing stable confidence, challenge seeking and persistence" (Dweck, 1986, p. 1046).

This research suggests that the dispositions to learn can be threatened by too much emphasis on skilled performance in academically oriented curricula. Dweck (1986) notes that emphasizing performance "may well create the very conditions that have been found to undermine intrinsic interest" (p.1042). We advocate including project work as part of the early childhood curriculum because it can provide a context that focuses on what individuals and groups can learn while exploring topics together.

Social dispositions. Parents and teachers are also concerned about strengthening dispositions related to social competence, for example, helpfulness, charitableness, and appreciation of others' efforts. These dispositions must first be elicited and acknowledged if they are to be strengthened. An effective way to do so is through project work, which provides natural contexts for expressing the component behaviors of these dispositions, thus allowing them to be enacted appropriately and to be appreciated by others.

Ames and Ames (1984) have shown how the goal structure of the classroom affects children's responses in terms of social dispositions. The researchers point out that reward and goal structure is a pervasive feature of the classroom situation. The reward and goal structure "defines which goals students are to accomplish, how students are to be evaluated, and how students are to relate to each other and to the task" (p. 535). Ames and Ames identified three basic types of goal structures: competitive, cooperative, and individualistic, as well as hybrids of the three. In a *competitive* goal structure, "Students work against each other such that the probability of one student achieving goal or reward is reduced by the presence of capable others" (p. 536). In a *cooperative* goal structure, "The probability of one student receiving a reward is enhanced by the presence of capable others" (p. 536). In an *individualistic* goal structure, the probability of receiving a reward is unrelated to the capabilities of others. On the contrary, it involves "fusing of the person with the demands of the task such that the task itself becomes the goal" (p. 536).

As extensive research indicates, the individualistic and cooperative types are more likely to foster dispositions toward effort, mastery, and cooperativeness. These findings support the proposition that young children's dispositions to mastery, effort, and interest may be at risk in a program that fails to provide enough activities in which noncompetitive, individual, and cooperative achievements are valued. As children work on projects together, both individual and group efforts are stimulated, encouraged, and valued.

Teachers can strengthen desirable dispositions in several ways. One is to provide ample opportunity for their manifestation, followed by acknowledgment and appreciation. Another is to minimize extrinsic rewards and competitive goals and to give specific informative feedback rather than general feedback. The dispositions to be cooperative and charitable are unlikely to be well learned from instruction or from posters in which a smiling animal declares that happiness results when everyone gets along. Such dispositions are more likely to be strengthened when children cooperate during carefully planned group project work. Since emulating models may also be important, teachers themselves should show that they, too, are intrigued by phenomena worth learning more about.

Development of Feelings

Feelings are difficult to define precisely. For our purposes, however, we define them as subjective emotional or affective states. Educators and parents are concerned about the feelings children develop toward school and their many experiences within it. We generally want children to feel accepted, comfortable, and competent, that they belong to the class group and can contribute to shared experiences. Such feelings can be learned while interacting with significant others in the group.

We are especially concerned about the feelings many young children may acquire when academic skills are not sufficiently balanced with opportunities for spontaneous play and other informal activities. When an early childhood curriculum focuses on academic tasks excessively, many children are likely to be at risk in important ways.

Because academically oriented curricula tend to use a restricted range of teaching methods and materials, it is unlikely that all children in the group can be equally successful. As yet, no clear evidence indicates the optimum proportions of the groups capable of doing the required tasks. Nevertheless, it is reasonable to assume that teachers aim the tasks to the perceived average ability level of the group. We hypothesize that the knowledge and skills included will be at about the right level of difficulty for a half or a third of the children in a given group. For another fourth or third, the knowledge and skills are likely to be in their repertoires already. The remaining children may be unable to respond to the work effectively.

In a study of the learning experiences of six- and seven-year-olds in Britain, four researchers (Bennett, Desforges, Cockburn, & Wilkinson, 1984) reported that 40 percent of the high achieving children studied were assigned tasks below their ability, and 44 percent of the low achieving children were expected to undertake tasks too difficult for them (p. 215). In the classes studied, the tasks seemed unmatched to the abilities of most of the children. Such high percentages of mismatches between children's abilities and the work assigned to them are likely to engender stress, despair, or boredom.

From time to time and from place to place, the percentages of mismatches may vary. We suggest that, as long as a standard teaching method or a single set of learning tasks is used, significant proportions of children are condemned to fail. Failure has dynamic consequences, the full impact of which may not show during the early years. In principle, when a young child's confusion, misunderstanding, misconceptions, and other difficulties do not cause the teacher to modify the instruction, vary the materials, or otherwise to change her approach, the child may learn to feel helpless, hopeless, inadequate, and generally incompetent. Indeed, in such situations the child *is* incompetent.

Occasional feelings of incompetence may be benign. But when children have such feelings frequently, regularly—in other words, cumulatively—they are likely to learn to feel stupid and ultimately to give up. We refer to this self-attribution as *learned stupidity*. There is reason to believe that children tend to bring their behavior into line with their self-attributions (Grusec & Arnason, 1982). When college students are confused by the content of a lecture, they can and frequently do attribute their difficulty to the lecturer's incompetence. But *young* children cannot as yet decenter in the same way. They have to attribute their difficulties to their own inabilities (Dweck, 1986).

Some children may cope with feelings of incompetence by being disruptive; others may respond by redoubling their efforts. But the large majority of young children subjected to tasks too far beyond their competence and outside their own experiences eventually give up and become psychological dropouts. No doubt some give up sooner than others. Giving up is probably one of the less objectionable ways of coping. Such children are the victims of what we might call "academic burn-out." As Donaldson (1978) points out,

> In the first few years at school all appears to go very well. The children seem eager, lively, happy. . . . However, when we consider what has happened by the time the children reach adolescence, we are forced to recognize that the promise of the early years frequently remains unfulfilled. Large numbers leave school with the bitter taste of defeat in

them. . . . The problem then is to understand how something that begins so well can often end so badly. (pp. 13–14)

It is important to note that the processes leading to self-attribution of stupidity are not usually or easily discernible to teachers. For some time, young children remain remarkably willing to undertake any number of decontextualized, abstract, or even frivolous and superficial tasks. Their eagerness to please the teacher, their general good will toward her, and their desire to participate in the ongoing life of the class typically last through the first few years of school. As frequently observed, children in academically oriented early childhood education programs are so eager to answer a teacher's question that they raise their hands whether they know the answer or not, and often before she has even finished asking the question. A few years later, however, teachers of the same children regularly ask for help and suggestions about how to motivate them. As Bennett et al. (1984) point out on the basis of their study of mismatches between tasks and ability,

> In the short term, inappropriate work appeared to have little direct emotional or motivational consequences for children of this age [six and seven]. Although cognitive problems, which manifested themselves in unproductive or confusing learning experiences, were all too clearly apparent in the post task interviews, this cognitive confusion was masked from the teachers by the children's cheerfulness and industry. The teachers avoided the immediate consequences of such confusion by rewarding individual endeavour, and by restricting their considerations of children's work to the product, not the process of such work. (p. 215)

The mismatch between children's competences and the curriculum tasks offered has become especially problematic in kindergartens in the United States. For many reasons, there is a strong trend to take the curriculum that used to be introduced in the first grade and use it in kindergarten, the first formal school year in most schools (Entwisle, Alexander, Cadigan, & Pallas, 1987). A major reason for this so-called push-down phenomenon is the assumption that the steadily increasing proportion of children entering kindergarten with prior preschool experience prepares them to cope with basic academic skills sooner than previous generations of kindergartners (Shepard & Smith, in press). Another reason for this practice is the tendency to overestimate children's academic ability and to underestimate their intellectual capacities. The push-down phenomenon has been accompanied by the widespread development of alternative classes for children who score below specified levels on tests of readiness required before kindergarten.

Although alternative classes are an attempt to minimize the mismatch between the curriculum and the capablities of kindergartners, they create new problems that could be addressed by including project work (Katz et al., 1986). When opportunities to work on projects are balanced with appropriate academic exercises, all children can be encouraged to participate in classroom life in accord with their individual readiness. In a given kindergarten, for example, some of the children will work exclusively on projects; others can profitably spend part of their time on formal academic exercises. Periodically the teacher can assess the project group's readiness to join the other group. Including projects in the daily work of the whole group alleviates the pressure on all children to succeed at the same tasks at the same time. All children can thus learn to feel competent and that they belong to the class and can contribute effectively to its activities.

IMPLICATIONS OF CURRICULUM RESEARCH

The discussion above focused on the effects that various teaching and curriculum strategies have on children's acquisition of knowledge, skills, dispositions, and feelings. In this section we discuss more general aspects of children's development and learning.

The Role of Interaction in Learning

Social competence develops in the course of interaction with others. However, intellectual development is also facilitated by interaction (Azmitia, 1988; Brown & Campione, 1984; Bruner, 1985; Glaser, 1984; Karmiloff-Smith, 1984; Nelson, 1985; Rogoff, 1982; Slavin, 1987a, 1987b, 1987c). Rogoff (1982) points out that "cognitive development depends on children's adapting and adopting the intellectual tools and skills of the larger sociocultural context, aided by other people" (p. 154). Young children's intellectual development is probably best served by opportunities to interact with adults, each other, the environment, and a variety of materials.

The younger the children, the more likely it is that interaction facilitates learning. This principle implies that young children should be engaged in more active and expressive processes than in passive and receptive ones. For this reason, many children benefit from being introduced to writing before reading, because writing involves more action and expression than reading does. Selected interactive computer programs can also be appropriate in the early years, even before children's writing and reading skills are fully developed.

Interaction cannot occur in a vacuum, however. Something of interest and concern to the interactors is required to sustain interaction. The relevant principle of practice is that sustained interaction requires content that is relevant, vivid, engaging, significant, and meaningful to the participants.

In classrooms dominated by formal academic instruction, much of the interaction is taken up with directions and instructions. The content of interaction is likely to be procedural rather than substantive, addressing matters of routines and directions (see Willes, 1983). Pupils' attention is drawn more to how to behave than to the content of what is to be learned. The work of Dweck (1986, 1987) suggests that emphasis on performance outcomes orients children internally toward their own abilities and how they are judged by others, whereas activities with learning outcomes orient them to the topic and work at hand. Similarly, Ames and Ames (1984) showed that, when the goals of tasks are set for cooperative or noncompetitive individual rewards and achievement, children approach the tasks in terms of the knowledge and effort necessary to proceed. Under competitive conditions, children become distracted by concerns about where they stand with respect to classmates. This body of research confirms the following view: When a curriculum is organized primarily around formal instruction for the whole group, the content of interaction among pupils and between pupils and their teachers revolves around matters other than substantive learning.

By its very nature, group life in school requires some classroom procedures. The practical issue, especially in the early years, is to ensure that procedures and routines serve the knowledge and skills to be learned. As a principle of practice, then, programs for young children should adopt only those procedures necessary to ensure that the really mind-engaging activities can occur. There is an optimum number of rules and routines: having too many results in the content of interaction being dominated by nonintellectual concerns; having too few may result in confusion or chaos. An optimum amount of routine and order is liberating.

Another principle of practice in early childhood education is that the younger the children, the more the content of interaction should relate to their own firsthand experiences and real environment. With increasing age and experience, children can and should be encouraged to develop their understanding of indirect experiences. In the later years, the content of interaction can be broadened to include the experiences and environments of others, those at a distance and from the past. During the early years, however, the content of interaction and activity is likely to engage children's minds when it is related to what is salient and familiar to them. As Carey (1986) points out, children gain understanding by relating what they are learning to what they already know. This is the cognitive rather than motivational reason for studying topics that are relevant to children's experiences.

The Value of Informality

Helping children acquire a fuller understanding of their experiences means that contexts should be provided so that children can reveal their understanding. These revelations help the teacher know which understandings should be developed, refined, corrected, or improved. The underlying principle is that the more informal the learning environment, the greater the teacher's access to the learners' representations, understandings, and misunderstandings. A related principle is that the better informed teachers are about these aspects of children's thinking, the better able they are to make appropriate curriculum decisions. However, *optimum* rather than maximum or minimum informality is recommended. Too much informality may slow down children's progress through the intended learnings, and not enough informality cuts off teachers' sources of information that could be used in planning.

The principle of optimum informality suggests a related principle of practice: children should be equipped with strategies they can use to let their teachers know of their confusions and questions. Thus children can be encouraged to say, "Would you explain it again?" "I'm lost!" "Can you help me with this?" "Is this what you mean?" "May I do another one? I understand it better now."

Children can also be helped to evaluate their own work. In American schools, children commonly take the products of their work home every day. This practice places undue emphasis on one-shot tasks and individual products. Instead, children could collect their work in a portfolio and at the end of a week or so select one piece they especially like. Their disposition to evaluate their own efforts could then be strengthened. On the basis of such self-evaluations, they might wish to repeat a task, do it differently, or elaborate upon it. If the curriculum is flexible and optimally informal, the teacher will have enough time and opportunity to participate in the evaluation process and to respond appropriately.

With optimum informality, teachers also have access to children's knowledge and understanding by observing and listening to them at play. Montessori long ago alerted teachers to the importance of observation as a way to learn about children's growing and "absorbent minds." But observation is not an end in itself. Its function is to obtain the kind of information that can serve as a basis for a wide variety of teaching and curriculum decisions.

The informal part of a curriculum can include two types of activity: spontaneous play and project work. Spontaneous play is stimulated and encouraged by the array of materials and equipment typically available in nursery and kindergarten classes. Blocks, dress-up clothes, easels, sandboxes, and many other items can be counted on to elicit and facilitate the young child's disposition to play. The body of research supporting the contribution of play to all major aspects of children's development continues to grow (see Bretherton, 1984; Fein & Rivkin, 1986; Garvey, 1983). Although informal, project work differs from spontaneous play because the activities are more purposeful, and the teacher has an important role in guiding and facilitating the work undertaken.

VARIETY OF TEACHING METHODS

Early childhood programs that emphasize basic academic skills tend to use a single teaching method and a narrow curriculum. A single teaching method is a *homogeneous treatment*. For a group of children of diverse backgrounds and developmental patterns, a homogeneous treatment is bound to produce *heterogeneous outcomes*.

Needless to say, we want some outcomes of education to be heterogeneous. Our goal is not that children become alike in all respects; differences in abilities and talents are valued in most communities. But many outcomes with respect to knowledge, skills, dispositions, and feelings should be homogeneous, that is, we want those outcomes for all children. That all children should have the disposition to be readers, for example, requires heterogeneous treatments. In other words, to achieve the *same* objectives with diverse children, *different* teaching strategies and curriculum elements are called for. This principle is based on two assumptions. First, the younger the pupils, the less likely they are to have been socialized into a standard way of responding to their environment. Second, the younger the pupils, the more likely it is that their background experiences are unique and idiosyncratic rather than common and shared. If homogeneous outcomes are best achieved by heterogeneous treatments, it follows that when a single teaching method is used for a diverse group, a significant proportion is likely to fail.

A related principle is that the younger the children, the greater should be the variety of teaching methods (Durkin, 1980; see also

Nelson & Seidman, 1984). For stability and practicality, however, the variety of teaching methods that can be used in particular contexts is likely be somewhat limited.

Heterogeneous Ability and Age Grouping

Teachers who use a single teaching method or restricted curriculum usually attempt to deal with heterogeneity by assigning children to ability groups. In the early years, this practice may create more problems than it solves. In the first place, obtaining accurate and reliable measures of young children's true abilities is difficult at best. They have had little or no experience in testlike situations. Obtaining a representative or large enough sample of their behavior across a wide enough range of their typical functioning takes both time and patience. Such being the case, the younger the children, the greater the chance that many will be falsely classified as "low" or "slow." In addition, since the rate of development and children's experiential backgrounds vary, some children may be labeled "low" or "slow," when perhaps within a short time the assessed behavior will change. As long as a standard measure is applied to a group, some scores will be lower than others. But the earlier children are tested, the greater the risk of mistaking poor performance (pseudo-slowness) for a true learning disability.

Furthermore, grouping by ability presents other hazards (Slavin, 1987a, 1987b). There is a strong tendency for the "slow" children to slow each other down (Wisconsin Center for Educational Research, 1984). Many teachers report that, when slow children are grouped together, they tend to drift, daydream, or interact unproductively. There is cause to be concerned about the top ability groups as well. Able children tend to speed each other up, and many among them experience considerable stress and anxiety about the danger of "falling out" of the group. Furthermore, even young children are aware of which group they are in and assess their own competence accordingly. Once a child has been labeled as "slow" and has internalized slowness as self-attribution, the label may have a cumulative effect and the chances of discarding the label are small.

The practice of segregating children by ability in early childhood programs seems to be spreading. At the same time, evidence is accumulating on the rich educative potential of mixed ability and mixed age grouping (Mounts & Roopnarine, 1987; Slavin, 1987a, 1987b). In a review of research on mixed age groups, Lougee and Graziano (no date) point out that mixed grouping also has many advantages for the development of social competence. Lougee and Graziano cite a report to the effect that, when some disruptive children were casually asked to remind younger children about the rules, they too became observant of them, presumably identifying with the teacher's role. Mounts and Roopnarine (1987) and Howes (1986) have shown that younger children engage in more complex play when grouped with older children. Apparently, small children can participate even though they are unable to initiate more complex activities themselves.

In a related experiment, Tudge (1986) reported on children being assigned tasks in pairs. If one child has the relevant concept and the other does not, the latter will learn from the former. However, learning occurs only if the child with the concept has a firm and confident enough understanding of it to explain it to the other in various ways and to resist regressing to the level of the other. The data also show that learning occurred only in those pairs who exchanged differences of opinion and argued about how to solve the problems in the task. An experiment in which pairs of preschool children worked on a complex block-building task demonstrated that, when the "novice" builders were paired with the "expert" builders, significant improvements in their performance carried over to subsequent tasks (Azmitia, 1988).

Virtually all projects can include enough variety of tasks to accommodate the diverse contributions from mixed groups. Project work gives younger children the chance to observe and learn the more sophisticated skills and knowledge of the older children. Similarly, older children can strengthen their own understanding by teaching younger ones (Benware & Deci, 1984).

Curriculum Research

Research on the long-term effects of different kinds of early childhood curricula supports the view put forward here: The curriculum should provide interaction, active rather than passive activities, and ample opportunity to initiate and be engaged in interesting activities (Karnes et al., 1983; Schweinhart et al., 1986a). According to Walberg (1984), a synthesis of 153 studies of open education, including 90 dissertations, indicated that, while children in open education were no different from others in achievement, locus of control, self-concept, and anxiety, they were at an advantage in their attitudes toward schools and teachers, curiosity, and general mental ability. They also had an advantage in cooperativeness, creativity, and independence. Walberg adds,

> Thus students in open classes do no worse in standardized achievement and slightly to moderately better on several outcomes that educators, parents and students hold to be of great value. (p. 25)

Fry and Addington (1984) followed children for two years after they had been in open and in traditional kindergarten programs. Compared with children from the traditional classes, those from the open curriculum performed better on social problem-solving skills two years following their kindergarten experiences.

Koester and Farley (1982) examined the effects of open and traditional classes on children diagnosed as either high or low on a physiological measure of "internal arousal." Children who are low on measures of internal arousal are commonly classified as hyperactive. It is assumed that they are hyperactive because their low levels of internal arousal cause them to provoke the external environment into being source of stimulation that can raise their own arousal levels. But contrary to common sense, as Koester and Farley found, hyperactive children placed in an open curriculum fared much better than in a traditional one. According to the interpretation offered by the experimenters, the informal curriculum provided hyperactive children a sufficient external source of arousal so that they were not compelled to disrupt the environment to create arousal for themselves. In the traditional formal curriculum, the level of external stimulation was so low that the children created stimulation by their hyperactive behavior.

A rich body of research on curriculum approaches designed for *cooperative learning* (Johnson & Johnson, 1985; Johnson, Holubec, & Roy, 1984; Krathwohl, 1985; Slavin, 1983) provides compelling evidence that long-term academic and dispositional outcomes are achieved when children are taught in groups that are mixed in ability, age, ethnic, and socioeconomic background and that are oriented toward cooperative goals. Consistent with research outlined earlier, Johnson and Johnson (1985) point out that cooperative learning experiences "tend to promote higher motivation to learn, especially intrinsic motivation . . . more positive attitudes toward the instructional experiences and the instructors" (p.23), and higher academic achievement than competitive or individualistically oriented classes. In addition, cooperative learning is associated with

> higher levels of self-esteem and healthier processes for deriving conclusions about one's self-worth . . . and result in stronger perceptions that other students care about how much one learns, and that other students want to provide assistance (p. 23).

SUMMARY

Including project work in the early childhood curriculum is neither new nor revolutionary. Several variations of it have been used by many teachers in many countries for a long time (Zimilies, 1987). Although some schools always maintain it as part of their curriculum, its wider use appears to come and go as ideologies and national priorities fluctuate. Our reassertion of its potential value to education in the early years is based on our understanding of contemporary research on the complex processes of development in young children. It seems reasonably clear that formal instruction in the early years may serve normative ends at the expense of the dynamic long-term aims of education. Given what is being learned about the nature and acquisition of knowledge, we suggest the principle that the younger the children, the more informal and integrated the curriculum should be.

Project work takes into account the acquisition of knowledge, skills, dispositions, and feelings. It can provide learning situations in which context and content-enriched interactions and conversations can occur about matters familiar to the children. Project work can provide activities in which children of many different ability levels can contribute to the ongoing life and work of the group. Working together on projects also provides situations and events in which social skills are functional and can be strengthened. Because project topics are drawn from children's interests and familiar environments, the knowledge acquired can have real cultural relevance for them. Last but not least, we advocate the project approach because it provides continuous challenges for teachers and thus can contribute to making the teacher's work interesting and professionally satisfying.

Chapter 3

Project Work in Action

For readers who are unfamiliar with the project approach, this chapter presents illustrations of how projects on a few topics might look. Some of the illustrations come from our direct experiences with teachers and children; others are based on reports. Before presenting the illustrations, we explain why we address the project approach for children from four to eight years old.

FIVE-YEAR AGE SPAN

We address the project approach for a relatively wide age range—four to eight years—in a single volume for three reasons. First, those who study and work with children in this range usually see it as a period in which intellectual development progresses at a rapid rate. Although continuous, development is also uneven; it progresses in spurts and lingers occasionally on plateaux. Furthermore, development is typically idiosyncratic, varying with the individual characteristics, circumstances, and experiences of the child. The project approach takes into account the unevenness of development by enabling children to undertake open-ended tasks alongside one another at varying levels of complexity and with equally acceptable alternative outcomes. Consider, for example, a project in which five-year-olds investigate the distance that different balls roll freely after rolling down a slope. One child is just able to release the balls, while another has the knowledge and skills to measure the distance. Both children participate and contribute to the task. Age itself is at best a rough predictor of children's capabilities.

Second, the project approach lends itself particularly well to teaching children of different ages in one setting. In many early childhood settings around the world, teachers work with groups mixed in age as well as in ability. The project approach is particularly suited to capitalizing on the differences among the children in mixed groups.

Third, we especially want to emphasize how the same topics can be fruitfully studied by children from four to eight years of age in accord with their developing intellectual and social competences. As children's knowledge and skills accumulate and develop, the work grows in depth, complexity, and sophistication. Thus, for example, kindergarten teachers need not be concerned if their pupils have already studied the weather in their preschool classes. Throughout early childhood, projects on most topics can be undertaken in such a way that knowledge and understanding continue to deepen.

In the project work described below, children of varying ages and abilities are able to work together, contributing to the group effort, studying the same topic continuously, extending and deepening their knowledge of it, and increasing the skillfulness of their work.

PROJECTS ON GOING SHOPPING

Most preschool children have occasionally gone shopping. By the time they reach primary school age, they probably have visited many shops and have made their own purchases. Although shops around the world vary considerably, it is likely that at least one child in a class of children with diverse backgrounds is familiar with the most unusual kind of shop.

At the beginning of a shopping project, dramatic play and discussion reveal children's widely varied experiences with shops. In early discussions, children are encouraged to tell what they know about the event, the shops they visit, and where food and other goods are usually purchased. Most children are able to tell their classmates about going shopping with parents or friends. Written accounts of shopping trips can be put into a class book and illustrated with drawings and paintings. The teacher can write captions for the younger children. Many of the older ones can write their own captions or stories and may even label drawings for those not yet able to write.

From the beginning of the project, the children can plan to set up a shop in the play area of the classroom. At first the props will be simple—shelves, a few items to buy or sell, a counter, cash register, shopping carts, baskets, and money. As the work progresses, more props will be added. Children can make signs denoting departments for various goods. Their understanding of money can be developed and enriched throughout the project. Those who already understand pricing may want to announce sales. Depending on ability, each child will use numbers at different levels of complexity.

The children can also visit a local supermarket, bicycle repair shop, fish market, open-air market, plant nursery, or garden center. The choice will depend on the opportunities afforded by the community where the school is located. In a town in China, for example, the children can visit a vegetable stall in a neighborhood market. During preliminary group discussions, the teacher can help them plan questions to ask the salesperson. Depending on the ages of the children, they can ask salespeople how they got the vegetables, which ones are weighed when sold, which are sold singly or by the dozen, which sell best, which perish fastest, and which last longest. The children can discuss which vegetables and fruits have to be peeled, cleaned, or cooked; which are eaten raw; and which items cost most and least. The children can bring some items back to school and begin to classify them (leafy, juicy, hard or soft, sweet or sour, with or without seeds, smelly). They can appreciate the idea of pricing and selling by weight and note the different kinds of scales used for lighter and heavier goods.

The visit brings new life to the classroom shop. The children may decide to set up a market of stalls with facsimiles of items for sale, a weighing scale, and money for transactions. The visit can also stimulate a wealth of drawings, paintings, models, graphs, diagrams, written reports and stories, and calculations. Individuals can work alone, or pairs and groups may want to collaborate. The teacher of younger children can help each group prepare paintings and drawings so that they can report what they learned to other groups who visited different market stalls such as clothing or housewares. The work produced can be displayed.

As the project unfolds, dramatic play is enhanced by the terms learned on a visit to a real shop and from real shopworkers. Additional props reflecting the newly acquired information can enrich dramatic play. The children "use" stock books, order books, sales slips, receipts for deliveries from the wholesaler, and they record customers' purchases. The complexity of the dramatic play will depend to a great extent on the level of understanding and background experience of the children involved. In a group of mixed ability and experience, the participants can take simple or more complex roles. Thus children whose understanding is more limited can learn by observing, playing, and working alongside more knowledgeable classmates.

A small group of preschoolers in India visited a bicycle repair shop set up on a nearby sidewalk. Although most of the children had passed by the shop every day on their way to and from the school, their attention had never before been drawn to it. They asked the repairman about his tools, the materials used for repairs, and what kind of repairs were common. He gave them some old pedals, tools, and bits of bicycle chain to take back to their class, where they set up a repair shop. Role playing continued for about a week, with some children riding tricyles and getting them repaired. During the dramatic play, some of the children became interested in license plates and made some to attach to tricyles and wagons. The project could have been extended to a gas station by visiting one in the neighborhood, collecting used tools and materials, and constructing a station in the schoolyard.

If supermarkets are common, a visit to one in the neighborhood can be planned in detail. The planning includes telling the workers beforehand about the goals of the project and the characteristics of the children. The teacher and children discuss which aspects of the supermarket to look at closely. The children can investigate many features that will help them understand how the supermarket operates and what the workers do there.

In a study of what shop assistants do, the older children can learn about sales, stocking the shelves, pricing, storing fresh deliveries, and moving goods from one part of the shop to another. Most supermarkets have large docks where goods are delivered. The children can inspect the dollies, trolleys, or other special equipment used for unloading and moving large piles of cartons. The children can make a list of the equipment used for lifting and transporting goods within the shop and examine how the equipment works.

They can also learn about the store and the stockrooms. They can note the contrasting temperatures of the shopping aisles, refrigerators, and freezers, and they can find out which items must be stored cold. In studying a department store, the children can sort the wide variety of goods into different categories and discuss the relative merits of their ideas. Activities such as pricing, comparing temperatures, and sorting merchandise can deepen children's understanding of the uses of mathematical operations and strengthen their skills in applying their own developing numerical recording.

The children's vocabularies grow as they become familiar with terms such as *taking stock* and *stocking up* and what it means when something is *out of stock* or *running out*. Children can be encouraged to ponder the distinctions among the terms *shop, store, supermarket, department store, market, shopping mall, shopping arcade, trading post, kiosk, bazaar,* and *boutique,* as appropriate to their experience and environment.

If the class is large enough that small groups need to be formed, each group can be responsible for identifying particular kinds of items to look at (e.g., house-cleaning items, produce, breads, canned goods, dairy products, beverages). The children can ask clerks which items are sold most often, what they cost, who marks the prices, why some are refrigerated, and anything else they would like to know.

The children can transform their simple classroom shop into a supermarket by adding more sale items, cash registers, bags, and so forth. "Zooming in" on particular aspects of packaging goods, some children can take responsibility for stocking the classroom supermarket with items sold in sacks, boxes, waxed cartons, plastic and glass bottles, squeeze bottles, tins and cans, and plastic and paper bags. The collections can include goods wrapped in paper, foil, transparent plastic, styrofoam, corrugated cardboard (for light bulbs), crates, net bags, and tubes (for ointment and toothpaste). The stock can also include a magazine and newspaper rack.

While some children will act out roles of workers within the supermarket, others will deliver goods from big trucks, and still others will gladly be shoppers. During dramatic play, if someone's car or bicycle breaks down, a gas station and garage mechanic may need to be added. As a project on shopping progresses, children may change the type of shop or add another part to it. More specialized props can be added to stimulate more complex play.

The classroom studies may diverge somewhat at this stage as children extend their understanding and branch out to related topics. Alternative perspectives may be taken to help children reach a fuller understanding of the process of shopping and the interdependence of customer, retailer, truck driver, farmer, and so on. For instance, the customer's point of view in the shopping event might be more fully explored. Customers in the class shop might be interviewed for their views of the facilities and services offered: getting to the shop, car parking, opening hours, bags for carrying purchases, the right to return damaged or unsatisfactory items, and attractive window displays.

In one school, a class of five-year-olds collected plastic shopping bags. They experimented with them by carrying heavy items across the school playground to determine which kinds of handles were best designed for comfort. Group members were then surveyed to find out their preferences. One kind of handle was clearly favored by most of the children. Following such an experiment, children may decide to compose a report and send it to the appropriate shop and manufacturer.

One kindergarten teacher reported that, when two salesclerks in the classroom supermarket ran out of money, they discussed the crisis together with great animation. They agreed that a bank was required. But lacking construction materials on the spot, they built an imaginary bank with imaginary nails and hammers. They informed bank customers in no uncertain terms of the precise location of the entrance, counters, and tellers as they distributed imaginary money.

Throughout the life of such a project, stories and picture books on related topics can be introduced. The children can also collect their own paintings, and with the teacher's help they can make a book entitled "Going to the Market" or "A Visit to the Bicycle Repair Shop."

Older children can also look at a sequence of events in which the shop is only one part of the process of getting products to the customer. In a study of where products come from, they may look at the transformation of raw materials, for example, sheep's wool as it is transformed into fabric for clothes. From sheep to clothing store, the wool takes an interesting journey while being processed along the way. Perhaps the children's town has a cloth factory that loads bales onto barges for transporting the wool to another stage in the production chain. Even though somewhat remote from "going shopping," a visit to watch the loading process might be an effective way to elaborate the understanding of a few children whose interest needs additional stimulus. Digression from the main theme, undertaken in the last phase of a project, may serve to point the teacher and children toward the next project, for example, a study of different modes of transportation.

PROJECTS ON THE WEATHER

Preschool and school-age classes often include a time at the beginning of the daily session when children take note of the day's weather. At the preschool stage, the weather provides relatively few events to act out or few roles for dramatic play, but it surrounds all children and can be studied for a lifetime.

Depending on the local climate, the weather can affect children's lives more or less directly in many ways. A project on the weather is likely to be most engaging in environments where the weather changes fairly rapidly and varies visibly, at least from week to week. On the whole, this topic involves more investigation than dramatic play. Depending on the ages of the children in the group, the project can "zoom in" on specific subtopics such as heat, light, and clothing.

An initial discussion reveals the children's levels of awareness and understanding of the weather and how it affects daily life. Most preschoolers can talk about how the sun, rain, snow, and wind feel on the skin and about the sounds of storms, high winds, and heavy rain. Some will recall dark clouds and rainbows and their feelings upon seeing them. In many localities children talk about snowballs and snowmen, slipping on the ice, shivering in the cold, winter sports, and their experience with travel in the snow.

The project work can begin with paintings and drawings of their own impressions, recollections, and ideas about the weather. Children can be encouraged to illustrate hot sunny days, a clear starry sky, storm clouds, and rain. Older children will also write about events or adventures featuring weather conditions. Stories, poems, songs, and books about familiar experiences will further stimulate discussion. Books with pertinent new information can be introduced throughout the project.

Weather Forecasters

School-age children can play the roles of people in the meteorological office responsible for forecasting and recording the weather. They can play the weather person on television, using a large cardboard box with a TV screen "window" cut out of the front. For the background, the children can make a satellite picture, a radar map, and charts of statistics about maximum and minimum temperatures and the times of sunrise and sunset, each of which can be flipped out of the way as discussion of them ends.

Activities related to the weather can include daily observations of the brightness of sunshine, precipitation, wind, and temperature. Each of these can be depicted on cards reflecting gross categories of variation. Younger children can make small crayon drawings exemplifying sunshine or rainfall; these pictures can then be placed on a chart recording each day or each morning and afternoon. Older children can consider recording finer variations in the relative amounts of cloud, sun, precipitation, and so forth. They can plot the readings for a week or two or longer.

Weather variables can be plotted in broad terms such as "very sunny," "mostly cloudy," "sun and clouds," "thick fog," "damp," "frost," "dew." Similarly, the rain can be described as "heavy," "light," "sprinkles," and "drizzle." Written descriptive reports can also accompany the chart record. Duration can be described as "all day," "early morning," or "afternoon." Rate and amount of snowfall and size of snowflakes can be included where appropriate.

Temperature Studies

A group of preschool children might investigate temperatures, using a large thermometer next to which different shades of red parallel the degree markings (pale pink = 0 degrees Celsius to 3 degrees; deep red = 45 degrees to 48 degrees). The group can chart their "readings" at different locations indoors and outdoors and compare morning and noon temperatures. Older children can write about things that affect the temperature in different places, such as prevailing wind, time of day, sun, fog, and rainfall.

Temperature investigations can include studies of ice. Children can observe the rate at which icicles melt, and the investigation can include experiments to test predictions. For example, using icicles of different sizes brought into the classroom, the children can predict how much water each icicle will produce when it melts. Predictions and outcomes can then be recorded on a chart and discussed with classmates. Preschoolers can make ice cubes from water tinted with different colors and then predict which colored ice cube will melt first and last. The ice cubes can be wrapped in different kinds and thicknesses of fabric to see which ones will take longest to melt. The children's attention can also be drawn to how their classroom and their homes are heated, aired, or kept cool.

Older children can discuss the variables in the experiments with greater understanding of cause and effect than younger children can. They can also generally predict with greater precision and record their observations more fully.

Wind Studies

Detailed work can be carried on in groups that take responsibility for specific subtopics. The teacher can help a "wind study" group to make a windsock and to place various sizes of windmills or pinwheels around the school grounds. The group can also look for weather vanes around their neighborhood and places visited. They can be encouraged to make their own weather vane. Older children will be able to infer something about the force and direction of the wind by observing the smoke from a chimney or smokestack.

The "wind study" group can take responsibility for recording the force of wind at several locations. After making a few observations, younger children can make drawings on separate cards depicting how the windsock, pinwheels, and windmills look when the wind is strong, mild, and light and then place these cards on the chart. Older children will be able to make more precise recordings on a chart. This group might also look for books and stories about wind damage, tornadoes, cyclones, and hurricanes.

The weather investigation could branch out to the subject of kite flying, varieties of kites, and the construction of kites and paper planes. The youngest children can participate in these activities with various kinds of balloons. They can attach paper of different shapes to string to see how the paper flaps in the wind. Older children can more precisely analyze the variables relevant to the flying potential of different shapes. They can describe their trials and discoveries and write instructions telling someone else how to replicate their most successful flyer.

Shade and Shadow Studies

One group of children can investigate shade and shadows. The project can include charting the darkness–lightness and sharpness of shadows each day. Special objects and sticks can be placed around the school for observing the length and angle of shadows. Some of the older children in the group can experiment with translucent materials such as plastic wrapping of various colors. Or they can collect different colored sunglasses and predict and observe the effects of the differences on the sharpness, glare, and color of shadows. Older children with a good understanding of clock time can try to design a simple sundial. Some children might take responsibility for observing the kinds of awnings and shop window shades in the neighborhood or town and report their observations to the class.

Rain Studies

A group responsible for rain studies can experiment with different materials to see how waterproof they are. Children can be encouraged to predict which material will be the most or the least waterproof. The teacher can help them develop a simple graph for recording their predictions and results. This work can be followed by examining their raincoats, boots, shoes, and umbrellas. Another group can keep track of rainfall when it occurs. This might include checking puddles for size and depth. They might also make chalk marks around the edge of the puddles to observe how quickly they dry in shade and sunshine.

Animals

During the autumn, hibernating animals can be watched from a classroom window as they eat and store food for the winter. In the spring, the children can make the first sightings of animals and birds that have been hidden for some months. In the winter in many parts of the world, birds that have struggled to survive respond eagerly when the children offer them food and water daily outside a classroom window. The habits and food preferences of birds can be recorded. If the local museum has stuffed birds, perhaps they can be taken out on loan so that the children can study them closely and draw them from observation.

Climate

Climate is another subtopic of the weather. From an early age, children may well have heard something about the polar regions, deserts, and jungles. The prevailing weather in different climates highlights interesting phenomena of adaptation, ecology, camouflage, and migration. The importance of sanctuaries for protecting threatened wildlife can be discussed. Some children may want to know more about the satellites that provide the meteorological office with photographic data. Other children may want to concentrate on tornadoes, hurricanes, typhoons, sandstorms, avalanches, and tidal waves that occasionally take place around the world.

Sayings and Myths

There is a great deal of folklore about the weather. Some of the children can collect sayings about it: "Make hay while the sun shines." "Red sky in the morning, shepherd's warning; red sky at night, shepherd's delight." "Save for a rainy day." "It never rains but it pours." Some metaphorical expressions are of interest: "pouring rain," "driving rain," "sheets of rain," "it's raining cats and dogs," "pea souper" (Br. for thick fog). Children can also invent new figurative expressions for different kinds of weather conditions.

By definition, the weather is a difficult topic for project activities; undertaking and completing work on it literally depends on the weather! However, as the weather and seasons permit, groups can be invited to report their findings to others. The reporting process should allow for questions and suggestions from children participating in other parts of the weather project. The older children can discuss the weather that prevails in different seasons, and study the habits of animals that have to accommodate to these changes. This learning will draw heavily on books and films or slides because only one season can be studied at a time. However, the season, whether spring or autumn, should be studied firsthand.

PROJECTS ABOUT A CONSTRUCTION SITE

Most young children will be interested in a project on building, especially if there are construction sites in their neighborhood. While building methods and materials vary around the world, children can learn much about what builders do and what tools, equipment, and materials they use. In the process of finding out about builders and construction, children can learn about their own homes and neighborhoods. A project on this topic includes a variety of investigation, construction, and dramatic play activities.

Initial discussion reveals the children's current knowledge and understanding of how buildings are constructed and the extent of their exposure to the topic. The discussion can include children's ideas of the sequences in putting up a building—when the roof is put on, when stairs are built, when pipes are laid, and how these things are accomplished can be discussed. The children can reflect their present understanding in pictures and block building in the classroom. If some children live close to an active construction site, they can be asked to bring back reports and descriptions of the equipment and materials observed. Books and pictures of large building equipment and of construction workers are also useful in the early stages the project.

The children can also make a class book with drawings, paintings, and writing about their own houses and how these are constructed. They can take rubbings of the texture of the walls, showing whether the walls are made of bricks, stone, wood, or stucco. They can count the number of rooms, windows, and doors and note their shapes. They can ask questions of their parents about the construction of the house and how old it is.

A visit to a local building site can be an interesting source of questions and information. Planning a visit includes talking about what to look for and what to ask builders. The children can be encouraged to note the tools, equipment, and work clothes of the workers. Materials such as cables, wires, sand, cement, bricks, mortar, lumber, buckets, pipes, blowtorches, pneumatic drills, and scaffolding can be noted. Equipment such as dump trucks, cement trucks, earthmovers, bulldozers, and cranes will also interest the children. If the building is to be very large, visits can be made periodically to note the progress. A large construction site usually includes a workers' hut, which is likely to interest the children.

Parents or grandparents who work in one of the building trades can be invited to talk about their work and tools and to answer questions. It might be possible to borrow some tools for study in the classroom for a week or two. These can be examined closely, drawn, and written about. After visits to construction sites, the children can discuss making a building site of their own in the classroom. Small groups can focus on particular parts of the classoom's construction site.

One group can construct a cement truck from large crates, scrap wood, or packing boxes (e.g., from a washing machine or refrigerator). A steering wheel can be included in the driver's cabin. The truck can be painted and appropriate signs added. Children can also make props representing bags of cement. Other groups can build a bulldozer, dump truck, or crane.

Another group can build walls of bricks made from milk or egg cartons or other boxes of manageable size. The bricks can be pasted or taped together to make sturdy walls. The children can discuss how to make doors and windows. A small stepladder, wheelbarrow, shovel, trowel, plumb line, crash helmets, and heavy work clothes are useful props to include. A workers' hut can be constructed on the classroom site as well. One or two children may build a road and a parking lot for the new building.

Most children are interested in handling real materials. Real bricks—old and new, rough and smooth, larger and smaller, differently colored—can be collected and studied for their properties. Many children will find it fascinating to realize how heavy each brick is and how large they look close up when they seem so small in the context of a high wall. The children can make rubbings and drawings of the bricks. Differences in age, texture, size, and color of bricks offer interesting topics of discussion about how those differences affect the process of building. A brick factory, if the neighborhood has one, is also a very interesting place for children to visit. Books can be consulted on the development of brickmaking. Different kinds of roofing materials can be investigated: tiles of various kinds, slate, wood, and glass. A local museum or other historical site might provide older children with examples of early construction such as log cabins and sod houses.

Experiments can be designed by some of the older children to find out the insulation properties of different materials designed to protect houses from the cold of winter and the heat of summer. Insulation experiments can be carried out quite simply by timing the melting of ice cubes enclosed in the different materials. The findings of these experiments can be displayed on the walls above labeled exhibits of the different materials tested.

Buildings can be looked at in any amount of detail. For example, the space inside the building can be partitioned into rooms in various ways. Children can be alerted to the different kinds of connections between one room and the next. They can discuss how the function of different rooms might dictate building requirements. Children can note that doors and windows will have fastenings of various kinds. The mechanisms of locks that have been discarded or replaced can be studied in the classroom. Problem-solving activities might include designing alternative mechanisms for closing and locking. The children might study the very earliest examples of log cabin locks, which had an inside latch with string going out through a hole in the door so that the latch could also be operated from the outside. At night when the string was pulled in through the door, it could be opened only from the inside.

As the children build and make things for the project, their understanding of buildings and the work of the bricklayers, masons, glaziers, roofers, plumbers, electricians, and the foreman and engineers is developed. The children will become familiar with the types of workers and what each contributes to the building. Specific knowledge about construction materials will be enhanced. This developing knowledge can be applied to their own homes and their school building. Construction activities in the classroom also involve the use of fine motor skills. In the process of making bricks and building walls, the children can be alerted to their shapes and how to match brick sizes to make corners. Many problem-solving skills are likely to be called on during the processes required for constructing the site and its various elements.

The dramatic play stimulated by the topic provides a context for children to consolidate their new knowledge and to enact the various roles involved. The vehicles that children construct should be large enough for them to load and unload bricks and bags of cement. The vehicles should have cabins large enough for the drivers to get into and out of easily. Similarly, the workers' hut should be roomy enough so that workers can take their coffee breaks in comfort. Large-sized constructions enable the dramatic play to be sustained and productive for several weeks.

Two kindergarten teachers in a midwestern U.S. city engaged their pupils in a project they titled "Houses: How Are They Built?" The children visited five houses at different stages of construction adjacent to their school grounds. Excerpts from the teachers' journal noting the children's comments and questions are included in Appendix 1. The children's comments and questions reflect their interest in what they observed. Follow-up activities in the classroom may involve discussing what they saw, as well as building with a variety of materials that include foundations, window wells, posts, joists, and beams that they began to learn about from their talks with the builders.

SUMMARY

These descriptions of projects are intended to give some idea of what project work often looks like in action. The main events in project work are described: class discussion, dramatic play, investigations, field trips, visiting an expert, and real objects in the classroom display of work and findings. Well-planned project work provides a range of activities from which children can choose. As children become engaged in various aspects of project work, their teachers can identify opportunities to enhance their knowledge, improve their skills, strengthen worthwhile dispositions, and ensure healthy feelings about their lives in the community of learners.

In the next chapter, we analyze in more detail what occurs in the classroom during project work, and we describe more fully the role of the teacher in organizing class projects.

Chapter 4

Features of the Project Approach

In the previous chapter we tried to convey a picture of what project work looks like in the classroom before taking up the detailed considerations of how to make it happen. In this chapter we outline principal features of the project approach that underlie the projects illustrated in chapter 3.

The principal features discussed in this chapter concern the procedures involved in implementing the project approach. We begin by broadly categorizing different kinds of project topics. Then follows a discussion of *relevance* as one of the primary criteria for selecting topics for project work. Next, types of activities for learning are suggested, together with their relationship to basic skills and curriculum subjects.

A discussion of the benefits of genuine exercise of choice by the learner is followed by an overview of the teacher's role in creating the learning environment of the classroom. The chapter concludes with a time-scale perspective on projects and the characterization of the early, middle, and later phases the life of a project.

TOPICS FOR PROJECT WORK

Topics suitable for project work can be grouped in various ways. The following topics illustrate a basic grouping:

1. The children themselves:
    homes, babies, families, food, school bus, TV shows, toys, games

2. The local community:
    people, hospital, shops, building site, transport services, waterworks, fish market

3. Local events and current affairs:
   annual carnival or county fair, important anniversary, independence day, royal wedding, visit by a famous person

4. Place:
   neighborhood, roads, directions, landmarks, rivers, hills, woods, transport

5. Time:
   clocks, seasons, calendar, festivals, holidays, historical objects, historical events

6. Natural phenomena:
   weather, water, wind and air, plants, animals, mini-beasts, rocks, sea, dinosaurs

7. Content-free concepts:
   opposites, pattern, color, symmetry

8. General knowledge:
   deserts, ships and other vehicles, inventions, space travel, rivers

9. Miscellaneous:
   hats, black holes, puppets, math or book week

The topics listed begin with the children themselves and work outwards, as it were, from their immediate world to more remote phenomena. The first three groups of topics concern children and their local environment. The fourth, fifth, and sixth groups concern the knowledge and skills related to the concepts of place, time, and natural phenomena. These are basic to understanding in the curriculum areas of geography, history, and science.

The seventh group of topics concerns content-free concepts. Projects based on these concepts usually span shorter periods of time and can sometimes form a backdrop for other project work. In a project on winter, for example, the pattern of snow on a fence or the crystal formation in a snowflake will be more fully appreciated through observation skills sharpened by previous project work on patterns. Content-free projects are more likely to be fruitful for school-age children than for preschoolers.

The eighth group, general knowledge, offers topics that can involve children with more public and universal information and that are not necessarily neighborhood specific. For the youngest, these topics should be about phenomena that are vivid to children and should provide opportunities for action and interaction.

The miscellaneous topics in the last group are chosen at the children's request, perhaps following some personal interest of one child or a group of children. The categories are not all mutually exclusive. "Food," for example, may be featured in several of the groups, depending on the project's perspective (e.g., eating food, buying food, foods in different countries, celebration foods).

Clearly, the number of potential topics far exceeds the amount of time available to work on projects. No particular body of facts or knowledge need be covered through project work. Even though different groups of children may undertake different projects, similar learning will occur. For instance, studies of birds feeding, vehicles, or clothes offer opportunities for observing closely, labeling parts, counting and tallying (counting in groups), making bar charts, sorting according to different criteria, finding out about things from books, and recording information. These skills are being learned and practiced with every project undertaken, although the emphasis may vary from one topic to another.

Depending on the practices of each school, different people may choose topics for projects. Individual teachers may select topics for their own classes, or a school may have a policy of offering particular major projects in each grade each year. Groups of teachers may perceive different interests for their classes in urban or rural schools, in cold or hot climates, and according to different opportunities in the local environment (a coastal fishing village, a rural mountain community, a suburban neighborhood, or a downtown area of a large city). In the Caribbean islands, for instance, a wide variety of plants have different kinds of seedpods, which can form the basis of projects on plant growth and cultivation. The pods also provide opportunities for discussions of shape, size, color, and texture (see Appendix 2). Most of all, the pods offer the children the opportunity to closely observe the interesting natural phenomena found in profusion in their own environment.

SELECTING A PROJECT TOPIC

Teachers or schools formulating curriculum policies can select the content of a project, using various criteria. These include relevance of the topic to children's lives, availability of materials and equipment, and access to resources within the school and in the local community. Relevance, the primary criterion for selecting a topic, is discussed in this chapter. The practical implications of alternative topics follow in chapter 5.

Dearden (1984, p. 155) offers a set of four basic criteria of relevance that can be readily adapted to the selection of project work. These criteria are (1) the immediate applicability of the topic to children's daily lives, (2) the topic's contribution to a balanced school curriculum, (3) its likely value in preparing children for later life, and (4) the advantages to be gained from a study of the topic in school rather than elsewhere.

Dearden's first criterion of relevance concerns the extent to which a topic encourages the children's disposition to make sense of their own personal experience and of life around them and in their community. Studies undertaken in projects about the neighborhood, the natural environment, the schoolyard, or the weather can help children to think more deeply and understand more fully the significant phenomena observed every day. This criterion also concerns whether a topic has relevance outside school. If children study an aspect of their local neighborhood in a project, then school learning can be applicable and helpful outside school—as they walk home from school or go into a store or listen to adults talk among themselves, for example.

Second, the topic should offer children ways of extending their knowledge and developing their skills through a range of different types of project content. Some projects lend themselves easily to scientific exploration and others to geographical or historical study. One of the teacher's responsibilities in selecting project topics is to ensure opportunities for learning in a balance of curriculum areas over the whole school year. A project on the weather may be followed by one on animals. Both may have involved the children in a considerable amount of scientific investigation. The teacher may then want this work to be followed by a study of the town to balance the curriculum with social studies. Children may, for example, learn about local stores and transport facilities.

Third, as children get older, their teacher should be concerned that the project topic will be helpful in preparing them for later life. Children's school learning must relate to the demands that society will make on them as they become increasingly responsible members of it. It is possible, for example, to overemphasize fantasy and imagination in projects. Although a project on teddy bears can be fruitful in a limited way, the children's time might be more usefully spent discovering important and interesting facts in a study of the local hospital and medical services, a nearby river, or how roads are built. Here, too, it is a question of balance; topics concerned with fantasy certainly have their own contribution to make to children's intellectual development (Egan, 1985). Children who have very little exposure to fantasy material are likely to benefit from opportunities to explore fantasy themes. On the other hand, children who have had a surfeit of fantasy and little direct contact with their actual environment may gain much more from real-world knowledge (French, 1985). The teacher must use her own judgment to balance topics and types of content to optimize learning for a particular group of children.

Fourth, if important content and skills need to be learned in school, some project topics that children will learn about outside the school can be omitted. This criterion might apply, for example, to holidays and festivals that children are exposed to through television, other media, and community observances.

Dearden (1984) makes the point that these four criteria may sometimes pull in different directions. They can, however, be applied by the teacher according to her judgments of the children's development within their own culture and her best guesses about what they may face as adults.

PROJECT ACTIVITIES

The activities in project work can be broadly classified as investigations, constructions, and dramatic play. These three types are distinguished mainly by their purposes. Every major area of the curriculum can be addressed in all three types of project activities. As indicated below, project work includes activities related to both language arts and early mathematics and science. Most project topics also lend themselves to poetry, music, and movement activities.

Children use both receptive and active communication strategies in investigations. Receptive strategies include listening and reading. Active strategies involve the instrumental use of language in seeking information, for example by asking questions and looking things up in a book. Although dramatic play is likely to be the major activity of the youngest children, they can often participate in investigation and construction activities as well.

Investigation Activities

A variety of activities with the primary purpose of investigation draws on all of the ways that children obtain information and ideas. Investigation can involve active and receptive strategies. Active strategies include questioning, estimating, hypothesizing, experimenting, exploring, and manipulating objects. Receptive strategies used in investigations include observing, listening, reading, looking at pictures, watching experiments, feeling objects, examining and observing events and items related to a project.

In extending their knowledge and applying more advanced skills, children in the early school years increase the number and types of active and receptive strategies they can use in finding out about a topic. Their growing command of language enables them to understand a "whole" in terms of its parts and to appreciate the relations among the parts. Children become better able to articulate notions of cause and effect, correlation, and function ("What's that bit for?" "Why is this different on this side?" "What happens if you shake it?" "Will it go uphill?"). Estimating is an important skill for all children to develop, but older children can apply more sophisticated and refined measurement skills in their investigations than younger children can. Older children can also talk, read, and write more about their investigations.

Visits and field trips offer opportunities to meet and talk with experts. Helping children formulate questions to ask them is part of developing communicative competence. Observation involves learning through looking closely at things. Observations can be short-term or extended continuous strategies. Examples of short-term observations are watching a visitor's demonstration, examining a particular object, and visiting a dairy farm. Examples of continuous observation activities are observing and keeping records of the weather over a period of days, observing the sequential steps taken by workers putting a new roof on the classroom, keeping track of birds feeding, and recording the gradual weight gain of a baby animal in the classroom.

Construction Activies

Making things for dramatic play and display are usually significant parts of a preschool project. Among the activities usually included are woodworking, painting, drawing, cutting, pasting, and making props. Materials can include wood, heavy cardboard, boxes of all sizes, styrofoam, blocks, sticks, screens, and furniture. One group of four-year-olds constructed a large ambulance by combining big wooden crates, a discarded piece of staircase, half of an old door, and much cardboard. A steering wheel was added, and an old bed sheet was sewn to two old broomsticks to provide a stretcher. This construction involved carpentry, sawing heavy cardboard, sewing, and cutting out the wheels and windows from heavy construction cardboard. The ambulance was painted appropriate colors and included the red cross characteristic of the local ambulances. With much discussion and guidance from the teacher, the children produced a construction that stimulated rich dramatic play.

As their skill in fine manipulation grows, children's construction becomes more skillful and elaborate. In addition to making models large enough to play inside, older children can make models on a smaller scale for classroom displays. As children grow, they become increasingly eager to achieve precise correspondence between the parts of a model and the real object it represents. If young children regularly build models out of a variety of scrap materials, they become increasingly skilled at fitting awkwardly shaped parts together, adding refinements, and making an increasing number of working parts such as wheels that actually go around and cranes that really lift small objects.

Making and building things, constructing large and small models of objects, painting, drawing, and preparing displays are activities that require planning. The planning sessions are devoted to discussions about what is to be constructed, details to be included, relative size of the parts, and kinds of materials to be used. Discussions continue as children begin to identify and collect the materials they expect to use in experimenting with alternative solutions to the construction problems encountered.

The quality of children's constructions is enhanced by the investigations they carry out. As they learn more about the attributes of the objects being constructed, their models become more elaborate. Language arts activities provide the link between investigation and construction activities. Talking, writing, and reading help to clarify understandings and give children new information. Language related to the topic is practiced in conversing, discussing, or writing descriptively or analytically about the objects being constructed and the events surrounding their use. Much conversation concerns social negotiation and collaboration as individual children contribute to a group construction.

Mathematical and scientific concepts are also involved in construction. For example, children experience the order in which things must be done, the time required for paint to dry, the comparisons made in choosing the best material or shapes for additional parts. They experience the tension of string, the thickness and rigidity of cardboard, the tessellating properties of different shapes. The variables of shape, size, area, scale, surface, texture, and color are all relevant to the processes of construction. The skills of counting, estimating, and measuring are used with increasing accuracy and become more salient to children in the process of construction as they grow older.

Dramatic Play

This type of activity includes enacting roles associated with the project topic. The younger the children, the more central dramatic play is to the life of the project. Preschool children usually enter into role playing spontaneously and develop variations as they go along. In the school years, groups of children may want to discuss and plan some aspects of their role playing, such as what roles are to be played and how turns might be taken to enact them. Children can be encouraged to search for appropriate dress-up clothes and props at home and among relatives and friends.

Dramatic play helps children to integrate newly acquired information with what they already know. It enables participants to apply their new understandings appropriately in script representations. They can find out from interacting with other children where they differ in understanding and experiences. Differences among playmates offer a basis for further investigation. Language provides a link between dramatic play and the other types of project activity. During play, children explore feelings they attribute to the roles enacted and add a subjective, "first-person" perspective to their understanding of the events enacted.

Invariably, lively dramatic play includes exchanging suggestions, proposing next steps, taking turns, bargaining, negotiating, resolving conflicts, and compromising. The teacher can encourage children to participate in the role playing so that all have experience as both leaders and followers.

Dramatic play also includes dressing up, manipulating props, interacting with other role players, rearranging furniture and props, and participating in sequences of events. Children always negotiate who will play which roles on different occasions. The dramatic play frequently suggests a need to write more signs, to make and gather more props, thus stimulating resourcefulness. The changing features of the play area encourage experimentation with alternative ways of setting the scene and arranging the props.

Information gained from investigation activities stimulates both the construction and dramatic play. Very often the questions that children raise as they become engaged in construction give rise to further investigation activities. The new findings stimulate more construction and further enrich the dramatic play. In the course of dramatic play, the need for another construction may emerge. In this way, each type of activity included in project work stimulates the others in cycles of successive investigations, construction activity, and dramatic play.

The most productive projects for preschoolers are those on topics that offer many vivid, active roles to play. For example, a hospital project can accommodate a variety of role players: doctors, nurses, patients, ambulance attendants, and anxious relatives of the injured. In contrast, a project on autumn leaves provides limited possibilities for role playing and is unlikely to lead to sustained interest. An example of animated conversations among five year-olds in a well equipped hospital ward in the housekeeping corner is shown in Appendix 3.

LEARNING OPPORTUNITIES

Although we have separated the activities associated with project work into three categories, all three (investigation, construction, and dramatic play) can call for applying the basic academic skills and concepts included in standard curriculum areas in the school years. The language arts such as verbal expression, story-reading, and writing are used in all three categories of activity. Similarly, mathematics and science concepts and skills are employed as children engage in investigation, construction, and dramatic play. This chapter gives various examples of how learning in these areas can occur in project work. Project work also takes into account the four categories of learning goals discussed in chapter 2, namely, knowledge, skills, dispositions, and feelings. Each is discussed in turn below.

Knowledge

One of the main purposes of the project approach is to help children acquire new knowledge. While discussing and investigating, children pick up new information and concepts. They also add to their growing store of event and script knowledge. Some new components of familiar events are learned from other children. Similarly, constants and variations in common scripts are learned. For example, in a project on "going shopping," children explore the following questions: "What is the same about all of the shops in the main street?" and "In what ways do they differ from one another?" "Is a bank a shop?" Many misconceptions can be exposed and clarified as investigation, construction, and dramatic play proceed. New vocabulary is used and the meaning of familiar terms is clarified and enriched. Acting out roles strengthens children's knowledge of the topic, especially if debates occur about how they are to be played.

Skills

Intellectual, social, and physical skills can be enhanced through project work. Although young children may not yet be adept at discussion, they may develop some skill as they begin to talk about plans and the work to be undertaken. Much learning occurs if the discussions become animated with alternative views and conflicting opinions. During investigations, children's observation and questioning skills are applied and strengthened. Fine motor skills are required in various aspects of construction such as woodworking, using scissors, and cutting and sticking parts of models. Expressive skills are also enhanced as children render in paintings their impressions of familiar events and places associated with the topic. Problem-solving skills (e.g., how to depict a flashing light on the top of a police car) are often called for in the construction activities of a project. As suggested above, social skills involved in cooperative effort come into full use during construction activities, as well as during dramatic play.

Dispositions

Many dispositions can be strengthened in the course of project work. For instance, it cultivates the disposition to look more closely at objects and events that are already familiar. The disposition to be absorbed, interested, and involved over extended periods of time is also encouraged in project work. Investigation activities in particular can strengthen the disposition to ask adults questions that help children to achieve a fuller understanding of familiar objects and events. The disposition to take an experimental and problem-solving approach to activities can also be strengthened as the various parts of the project develop. Because project work focuses on learning rather than on performance, the dispositions toward effort, mastery, and challenge seeking can be developed.

Feelings

The variety of ways that children can contribute to project work enables the teacher to help each of them feel included in the life of the group. Such feelings are deepened as children express their appreciation for each other's contributions. As children consult with the teacher and with others, feelings of confidence in their own observations and questions also can develop. Parents' positive responses to children's requests for information and items for construction and dramatic play enhance feelings of continuity between home and school. The interest that parents express in children's reports of a project's progress also increase feelings of stability and community. Investigations of familiar events and places contribute to feelings of appreciation and respect for the work and the contribution and interdependence of many adults in the wider community.

CHILDREN MAKING CHOICES

Project work offers children the opportunity to make choices at several levels, each with different educational implications. Some choices are procedural, some aesthetic, and some functionally intrinsic to the activity. Choices have implications for learning in cognitive, aesthetic, social, emotional, and moral areas. Varying in importance, some choices may have no far-reaching effects, but others may result in the success or failure of a major effort. Some options may be freely available, while others may involve negotiating with the teacher.

Whatever the nature of the choice, the children can consult the teacher for advice, thus giving her an opportunity to talk with them about the work and to share her views and expectations. The practicalities of offering choices to children during project work can be thought of in terms of several options: choices concerning what to do, and when, where, and with whom to do it. Whether to do something and for what reasons are very often matters that the children negotiate with the teacher. Each of these questions is discussed below.

Choice About What Work to Do

There are clear limits to the extent that a child may choose not to undertake a given activity. A child cannot, for example, be allowed not to learn to read or write. However, many other more specific activities might be offered as genuine alternatives; similar tasks can often take very different forms. Writing a letter, a story, or factual description of an event may equally develop the skill of writing. A sequence of drawings with captions may be presented in a "concertina" (Br.) or accordion book, in a book with pages (Figure 1), or in a pie chart presentation of a cycle, (Figure 2).

The teacher must be alert to the range of activities that children undertake to ensure that they do not miss out on many enriching experiences. Children who regularly refuse to paint or to make models may need help overcoming their resistance, because we have reason to believe that young children benefit from acquiring a broad range of expressive skills. Refusals may present an occasion for the teacher to ask the child why he or she does not want to participate. In this way, children learn to become accountable for justifying and explaining their choices. Through project work, the teacher may be able to suggest alternative learning activities that can be undertaken in different ways for different purposes.

Choice About When to Work

Children can also choose when to carry out tasks. So long as a particular piece of work is undertaken within a given period, two days for example, a child may choose to do it sooner or later, at the beginning of

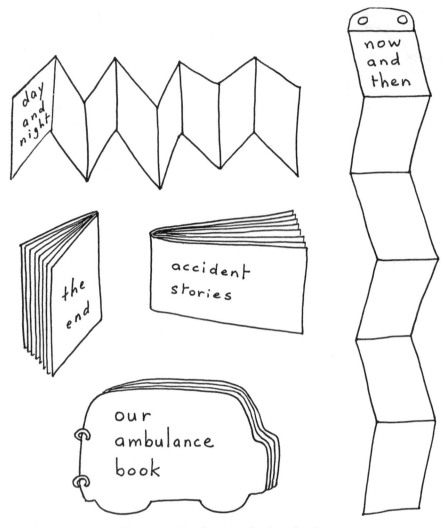

Figure 1.   Books to make in school.

the time period or towards the end. Each choice has advantages and disadvantages, which can be discussed with the children. Discussion may lead them to favor completing one task early and another one later. Sometimes a child may be among the first to attempt a piece of work; at another time the same child may prefer to wait and see what other children make of the task before attempting it themselves.

In one case where the teacher offered the children a fairly open assignment, some of them sought the challenge of having the first try,

Winter

Spring

Autumn

Summer

Figure 2.   Pie-chart representation of the seasons.

while others waited to build on the earlier attempts. From watching their classmates, those who waited learned alternative ways of approaching the activity. Because there were several different responses to the task, learning was much more than mere copying. Children who did copy, however, discussed which model to copy. The following detailed description of this example illustrates the kind of learning potential offered by many open-ended tasks.

The activity consisted of painting checkered flags on large pieces of white paper for props in a play. The first child produced an interesting abstract design of randomly placed rectangular black shapes of different sizes. Immediately after, a second child painted rows of black rectangles separated by white spaces. Two days later, third child painted alternate black and white squares row by row, producing the conventional checkered pattern. This child, a slow-moving and deliberate person, spoke to the teacher conspiratorially as she came to see him painting: "I have been thinking how I would do this," he said. No child spontaneously tried painting vertical and horizontal lines and subsequently filling the alternate squares or boxes, as an adult might approach the task. During the three days over which this activity was undertaken by different children, a considerable amount of mathematical language was used to describe and compare the products. Clearly, there was no single right way of carrying out the task.

On another occasion, a picture-map drawing activity that a few children had undertaken was discussed at the end of the day. Early the next morning, three of the children whose work had been discussed asked whether they might try it again. Their second attempts showed a marked progression in complexity and cohesion. Had they been required to wait until some later time before being allowed a second try, some of the interesting developments in their work might have been lost. Within the balance of activities, however, it was important to make sure over a week's time that these children did not spend a disproportionate amount of their time drawing, or if they did, that the same thing would not occur repeatedly.

Choice of Where to Work

Within one classroom, different kinds of space can be created for children to work in: lighter or darker, more open or more confined; facing other children, the wall, or window; working with a group of others or on one's own; standing, sitting up at a table, or lounging comfortably on cushions on the floor. Sometimes a direct relationship exists between the task and the chosen place, such as painting at an easel. On other occasions the relationship is not so direct; a piece of writing might be undertaken in an open area or in a small space, with or without other children close by.

Children can learn that alternative settings have different benefits to their work or to their mood at the time. Some children's choice of where to work is best curtailed for a period of time by the teacher. When the beneficial effects of working in different places is discussed with children, they can understand the reason for the teacher's advice or demand. General recognition of such alternatives helps children make thoughtful choices that support their efforts and facilitate their learning.

Choice of Co-workers

At this early age, friendships are constantly forming, developing, or breaking down under the pressures of classroom life. Important discoveries are being made about what is involved in friendship, communication, cooperation, collaboration, and conflict. Young children vary enormously in the range and quality of interpersonal experiences that they have had outside of school. Social difficulties that persist throughout the early years of schooling are likely to cause pain and to reduce the quality of life for a person during that time and perhaps for several decades beyond it.

Children can be greatly helped by teachers who offer alternative strategies for solving social problems. Through project work, children can develop social competence through opportunities to talk, work, and play together in the classroom. Cooperation and collaboration can be encouraged by presenting appropriate problems to children. Some children prefer to work privately on making a book of their own. For others, the work is undertaken with much more enthusiasm if it is prepared by a group to be presented as part of a display. The teacher can encourage children to work under both conditions, helping them to see the benefits to be derived from alternative working arrangements. The following account gives examples of activities requiring negotiation and collaboration.

After visiting a large local garden center (nursery), a class of six- and seven-year-old children was given a two-meter square of white cardboard (packing material pasted together with kitchen paper). The square was spread out on an area of the floor cleared for the purpose. The activity was preceded by a brief discussion of what the children had seen at the center and what items might be included in a large collaborative painting. Only three procedural instructions were given: (1) three children were to work together for a short period (unspecified), (2) each child was to paint one or two items in the total picture, and (3) each child was to give up his or her turn to another child who had not yet made a contribution. The children took their turns, shorter or longer ones, and painted their ideas in the available spaces, which became smaller as the work progressed.

At least two-thirds of the class participated in the activity. The final result showed the care taken to preserve the unity of the picture. The items, of which there were many, were roughly in proportion to each other and observed the general rules of spatial relations, such as above, below, at the side, and in front. Items included the closed-circuit TV monitor, the check-out counter, a set of patio furniture on display, and shelves of watering cans, gardening gloves, ornamental dried flowers, feather dusters, bug sprays, packets of seeds, sacks of compost, potted plants and cut flowers, and many figures representing customers and workers. The overall effect was movingly suggestive of the place the children had visited as a class on the previous day.

The teacher intervened only toward the end, not without some trepidation, to suggest that the children see what the picture would look like if they filled the gaps between the objects with a "wash" of some sort. They tried using a pale yellow ocher. The overall effect was remarkably pleasing, and the whole class was happy with the result. It must be said that this work was achieved later in the school year, after the children had developed social skills that facilitated collaboration in the classroom.

Examples of choice, such as those described above, are easier to observe in more informal classrooms where the curriculum is integrated. Teachers wishing to introduce this kind of informal work can find many helpful suggestions and a description of classrooms graded according to extent of informality and integration in J. Taylor's book, *Organising and Integrating the First School Day* (1983).

The project approach offers children a learning environment that develops their sense of their own competence and worth. It creates a classroom ethos in which children's points of view are taken seriously and their feelings and opinions treated respectfully. It offers the opportunity for children to try out their developing powers of judgment and to learn with confidence from their mistakes. The children's use of judgment can be practiced in situations calling for negotiation and decision making where genuine choices can be made. Choice is itself a neutral term, however. If the alternatives to choose from are of little educative value, then motivation is unlikely to be enhanced. The available alternatives must be carefully prepared and monitored by the teacher.

THE ROLE OF THE TEACHER

In chapter 1 we discussed the differences between project work and systematic instruction. The four distinctions listed in Table 1 (p. 11) have implications for the way that children interact with the teacher and with each other in class discussion. It is the teacher's responsibility to set clear expectations of work and conduct and a prevailing tone that facilitates the open exchange information.

Procedures are very important in the project approach because children work individually and in small groups over periods of several days or weeks. Thus children must be clear about the teacher's expectations of them. In contrast, systematic instruction generally calls for children to act in the short term, primarily in response to specific instructions. Young children need frequent reminders about the alternatives open to them, about what they should be doing, and about where, when, and with whom they should be doing it. These reminders are not always stated in the form of instructions. Many are expressed as suggestions or options to be considered by specific groups or individuals. Other reminders can take the form of examples referring to individuals who worked in a particularly successful way, who chose carefully, and who can talk about the reasons for their decisions. Children do not usually recount their experiences to show off or to intimidate other children, but to explain how they approached the problems they encountered. The older children's attention can often be drawn to the notices around the room, indicating what to do and how to set about doing it. Notices might be entitled: "Things you can do alone or with a friend," "Things to be finished before Thursday," and "How to mount your drawing." An example of how a notice entitled "How to make your own book" might look is given in Appendix 4.

The teacher can use many devices to strengthen the children's disposition to be resourceful and independent as they work on projects. For instance, the teacher can ensure that children have easy access to materials and equipment set out for them, that books and displays are readily available for them to consult for information, and that resources such as word banks are conveniently located around the classroom so that they can find words for their writing. During class discussion, children can be reminded of the procedures for helping themselves and each other when the teacher's attention is taken up elsewhere.

The second important aim of class discussion is to facilitate the exchange of information. In classrooms where projects are being developed, the free exchange of information contributes to the smooth running of the class. Here, the information emanates not only from the teacher, but also from children's reports of their own understanding and the progress they are making. Children can help one another a great deal by example and as consultants and collaborators. Since much of this work represents information, it can be displayed to serve as a resource for other children while they pursue their investigations. The teacher also has an important role to play in helping children appreciate each other's work.

CLASSROOM DISPLAYS

The teacher can use bulletin boards, classroom walls, and table surfaces to display information, children's work, collections of objects, lists of words, books to consult, instructions for procedures, and materials and equipment to work with. These displays help children to be more independent of the teacher as they work. Teachers who have experience working this way value the time thus released to observe and interact with children involved in dramatic play or to help with construction techniques. This approach also enables the teacher to move around the classroom for much of the time and to keep in touch with what all of the children are doing. The teacher can use the time to encourage their efforts and where appropriate to suggest ideas. In project work the teacher's role is more that of adviser and guide than instructor.

Over the course of a project, the teacher orchestrates the developments, collecting and displaying work products, presenting the progress of groups and individuals to the whole class by means of discussion and display. There is ongoing evaluation. Children can also accumulate their individual work in a project folder, which serves as a record of the project work accomplished.

PHASES OF PROJECT WORK

Projects can be described as having three general phases that typically merge into each other. Outlined briefly below, each phase is explained more fully in later chapters.

Phase I: Planning and Getting Started

A project can begin in several ways. Some begin when one or more of the children in a group express an interest in something that attracts their attention. Some projects begin when the teacher introduces a topic or when a topic is selected by agreement between the teacher and the children. A more detailed discussion on topic selection is presented in chapter 5.

The main thrust of the first phase of project work is to establish common ground among the participants by pooling the information, ideas, and experiences the children already have about the topic. The teacher can help them build a shared perspective. For instance, in the school bus project, the children discussed their experiences, noting those that were common to them all: waiting for the bus, climbing aboard, finding a seat, riding through the town, and getting off at the school. They also shared less common experiences such as being the first or the last to board the bus, just missing the bus and having to get to school some other way, the bus driver arguing with a policeman, and being on the bus the morning it broke down.

During preliminary discussions, the teacher encourages the children to talk about the topic, to play, and to depict their current understandings of it in other ways. The teacher acts as a source of advice and suggestions. Children are invited to bring pertinent objects from home and collect materials for the construction activities of the project. The children and teacher develop plans for conducting investigations, make arrangements for visits or visitors, and develop initial questions to be answered by the investigations. Procedures for obtaining construction materials are also worked out at this time. Some preliminary investigations upon which to build later ones might also be introduced during this phase. For example, a project about clothes might begin by taking a close look at the children's coats and noting colors, types of buttons, belts, and fabrics.

Phase II: Projects in Progress

The main emphasis during the second phase is on introducing new information. This is sometimes done by means of visits outside the school, sometimes by a visitor who talks or demonstrates special expertise, or by collecting real objects, books, photographs, or artifacts. For example, a group (or a whole class) of children studying shops or stores might visit nearby shops. The visit can include talking to the shopkeepers and buying some items for the class. This shared event provides a common background of experience on which to negotiate new understandings. The visit can enhance the realism with which the children play "shops" and "shopping" in the classroom. Visits also increase the likelihood that the children will ask for clarification of their perceptions of what they have experienced together.

In a hospital project, the teacher might arrange to have a nurse or a doctor talk with the children and leave them some spare instruments or X-rays as props for their play. The children explore the new sources of information, assimilate the new knowledge, and identify and revise misconceptions through interaction with their classmates and the teacher.

In the second phase of a project about going to school on the bus, the teacher might arrange for a detailed study of the bus itself and ask that it be brought to school earlier than usual so that the children can talk to the driver and inspect the different parts of the vehicle. They might build a bus in the classroom, or draw, paint, and write about the bus, its journeys to school, traffic regulations, the role of the police, the different modes of transport by which the children come to school, the distances and times that different children travel. The second phase, along with the first, gives children common script knowledge about going to school on the bus. They also learn about less common occurrences, dangers, and emergencies, as well as normal experiences and safety precautions.

An important role of the teacher during this phase is to encourage children's independent use of the skills they already have. These skills include observation, communication, drawing, and painting. Older children can apply their developing competence in writing, reading, and calculating. In this phase the teacher also attends to strengthening the children's dispositions to find out about or pursue a topic that interests them. The teacher provides materials and offers suggestions and advice about appropriate ways to represent their findings and ideas.

Phase III: Reflections and Conclusions

The main thrust of the third phase of project work is to help bring the project to completion with group and individual work and to summarize what has been learned. In the third phase it is hoped that most of the children will share a thorough understanding of the topic. Introducing new information at this time may be inadvisable. Instead, what is required is an elaboration of the children's learning so that its meaning is enhanced and made personal. We assume that as children apply their new knowledge they can make it truly their own.

For the older children, the third phase is a time of rehearsal and reflection on the new levels of understanding and knowledge acquired. They express their increased knowledge not only in play, but also in wall displays, music, drama and dance, class books, and folders of individual work. Sometimes a culminating activity can be organized so that children can present what they have learned to their classmates. They may invite their parents or children from other classes to see their work and explain what they have learned, how they learned it, and the procedures they used to develop the project.

For three- and four-year-olds, the third phase is usually a time for them to role-play in their project constructions. Thus, if they have built a doctor's office or a shop, this phase will consist mainly of enacting the various roles they associate with those settings. The social and dramatic play helps them to integrate their modified and fuller understanding of the real world.

In the third phase of the school bus project, the teacher can help children to elaborate their play with the bus they constructed. The class can discuss possible school bus stories for dramatic play: a story or play about the day the school bus had to go a different way because a tree had fallen across the road in a storm; or the day the children helped the driver change a flat tire. They can also dictate or write their stories. They can play or make up games, such as dice and board games in which the progress of the bus is hindered or facilitated along the way to school. They can make up new songs and poems about the bus if they have not done so already. They can make a pictorial story about the journey to school.

The Three Phases Illustrated in Dramatic Play

In dramatic play in the context of a project, children negotiate and refine their growing understanding by consulting with other children and the teacher. For example, in the first phase of the hospital project, prior understandings are expressed and shared in play. Early in the project, children might role-play their experiences of visits to the doctor, being ill at home, patching up grazed knee.

In the second phase, new information is tried out. The teacher may have read the children a story about a girl who broke her arm and had to go to the hospital, have it set in a plaster cast, and have the cast removed. The children might try out their newly acquired script information by acting out a visit to the hospital to have an injured arm X-rayed, followed by the succession of events as described in the story.

In the third phase, children consolidate new understandings. During the dramatic play of the third phase of a hospital project, the children may be happy to play various combinations of events: accidents involving broken bones, visits to the doctor's office and to the hospital to see the specialist, being X-rayed, having plaster casts put on and removed. In this more extended and elaborate play, old understandings are clarified and enriched by newly acquired script knowledge.

SUMMARY

The principal features of the project approach have been outlined in this chapter with practical examples. The analysis is intended to make more explicit what happens behind scenes such as those described in chapter 3. In many cases we have described events in the classrooms of teachers experienced in the project approach. Many teachers began to use this approach in a small way and extended their project work as they developed techniques that worked in their situation.

CHAPTER 5

Teacher Planning

Projects can be short-term undertakings or they might enliven a class-room for eight weeks or longer. Preschool children are likely to engage in less extensive projects than older children. However, throughout the early years, projects should vary in length and scope. Short-term, small-group, or spontaneously generated projects require little advanced teacher planning. Occasionally a project of this kind arises from an unexpected event such as the resurfacing of the schoolyard or bees swarming nearby. In such cases, advanced planning is impossible. However, if a project is to take several weeks and involve the whole class, advanced planning is essential. This chapter describes some techniques for outlining initial plans for the project and suggests ways to elaborate plans and adapt topics for particular groups of children.

SELECTING A TOPIC

As indicated in the previous chapter, the choice of topics for projects may be made by different people according to the practices of the school. Individual teachers may select topics for their classes, or schools may develop a policy of offering specific major projects in each grade each year. Teachers develop some projects on the basis of a social studies or science curriculum guide required by a school district (Amer.). Sometimes a whole school undertakes one project; the teachers plan as a team, and each class takes responsibility for a particular area or subtheme related to the main topic. Occasionally the children in a class select a topic, and the teacher helps them develop it and contributes to its scope in discussion with the children.

Once a suitable topic is selected, the teacher works out some provisional plans on paper. One technique teachers have adapted for this purpose is that of creating a "topic web." This is a diagram in which information is grouped under subtheme headings. The major advantage of a topic web is that the ideas can be generated in any order; no sequence is dictated by the form of the web. In that respect, it is different from a flow chart, which has a temporal sequence built into it.

MAKING A TOPIC WEB

A web is a mapping of the key ideas and concepts that a topic comprises and some of the major subthemes related to it. As teachers become more experienced, they map the topic area with a variety of available resources in mind. Teachers can of course work with a web designed by someone else. But the process itself brings the teacher face to face with her own personal knowledge resources. Some teachers inexperienced in the project approach have reported to us that brainstorming a topic web increased their awareness of how much they did or did not know about a topic before looking it up in a reference work. Teachers often report a tendency to underestimate their own knowledge and how much young children can learn from real objects, people, and places, as well as from books. The procedure outlined below is recommended for teachers who have had little or no experience in making a web.

PROCEDURE FOR CREATING A TOPIC WEB

Five steps are suggested for generating a project web:

1. Take approximately 100 small slips of paper of about ½ by 2 inches. Write down an idea related to the topic, each on a new slip of paper. For example, take the topic of "going to hospital." The first succession of ideas might run as follows: ambulance, stretcher, doctor, ward, X-ray, nurse, waiting room, receptionist, bed, operating theater, bandages, and syringes. Continue generating ideas in free-association fashion and writing them on slips of paper for about ten minutes (Figure 3).
    If this brainstorming exercise is conducted in a group, each person will probably produce the first set of ideas in a different order. Most of the participants will have similar ideas, but some ideas will be original, idiosyncratic, and unique.
2. Move the slips of paper around on a table so that like ideas are grouped together. Similar groups can be placed next to one another (Figure 4).

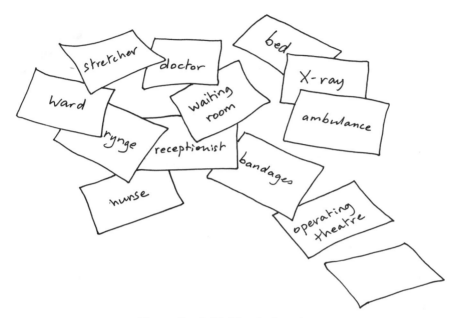

Figure 3.   Initial brainstorming.

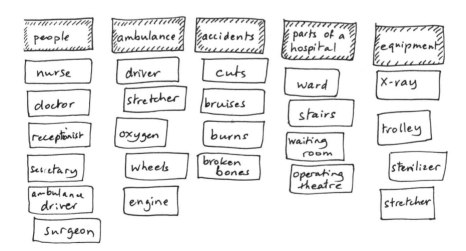

Figure 4.   Ordering the items and labeling categories.

3.   Take a few slips of paper of a different color. Write a label that gives a heading to each group. If one group is very large, usually the ideas can be separated into two or three smaller subgroups under the main heading and each subgroup given a heading. For the hospital topic, the headings might include accidents, parts of a hospital, the ambulance, hospital workers, and treatment equipment.

4.   If a group of teachers is brainstorming a web together, they can look at each other's ideas at this point in the process. Ideas that might enrich one's own web should be added to it. Sharing can be reassuring to individuals because the sets usually have much in common. It is also interesting, however, to observe the variety of ways others arrange ideas, yielding differences in focus or perspective on the same topic.

5.   At this point, the ideas should be transferred to one sheet of paper for a more permanent, initial record. The most flexible way to do so is to take a large sheet of paper and begin with the title of the topic in the center. Then draw short lines radiating from the title and write the labels given to each group of items. Lines can then be drawn to other

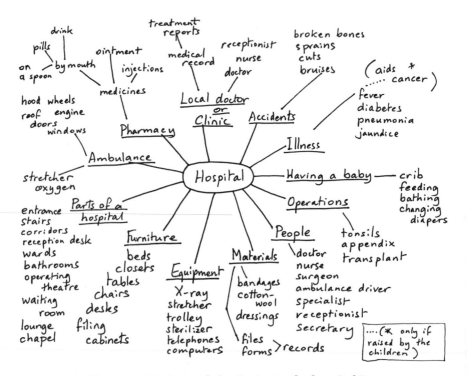

Figure 5.   Project web for "going to the hospital."

subheadings and eventually to lists of items in each group and sub-group (Figure 5). Examples of webs for projects on "going shopping," "weather," and "a construction site" described in chapter 3 are shown in Appendix 5.

It is generally a good idea at first to consider more ideas than could possibly be used in a single classroom project. In the first place, not all of the ideas generated by brainstorming will be suitable as areas of investigation by the children. Second, if a teacher has considered a wide range of possibilities by herself, it will be easier for her later on to incorporate the ideas that children may offer in a preliminary discussion.

POSSIBLE CURRICULUM AREAS

After the web is made, it is useful to produce a second web that organizes the project ideas into curriculum subject areas and the learning activities associated with them. Remember, however, that the curriculum subject web should be developed only *after* the first kind of brainstorming has been completed. This sequence minimizes the likelihood of distorting the topic itself toward setting tasks within conventional subject boundaries.

Appropriate learning goals for children are more likely to be addressed by using the brainstorming web, which reflects relationships among the items of information about the topic itself. The curriculum subject web, on the other hand, reflects the teacher's purposes, which may or may not correspond to the children's. For example, measuring the size of a vehicle involves exercising considerable mathematical skill. However, if the vehicle is measured only because the teacher wants the children to practice measurement, then it will be of much less value as a project activity than if the children do so to make a model roughly to scale. Making a model to understand how the vehicle works provides opportunities for practicing measurement skills, rather than the other way around.

DECIDING ON A PROJECT'S SCOPE

The more general and abstract a topic, the more scope it has for sub-dividing the content. With each subdivision, topics become smaller until they are microscopic. In the reverse direction, larger topics can be created by combining small, related topics. We suggest here that smaller and more specific topics are probably more suitable for younger children. As children get older, they can more easily see connections between subtopics within larger topics with a wider scope. Webs showing how the scope of a project on a school bus would vary for older and younger children are presented in Appendix 6.

One technique that narrows the focus of a topic is what we call "zooming in" on a subtopic in the web. It is usually possible to focus on specific subtopics in the same way that a camera with a zoom lens can focus on a close-up view of part of a subject. The subtopic titles then become the center of a new web, which can be as elaborate as the previous one on the main topic. For example, in a hospital web, the ambulance can become a "zoom." At the center of a new web, the ambulance can give rise to subtopics such as motor, wheels, emergency equipment, siren, flashing lights, materials, driver, emergencies, routes to the hospital, and shifts worked by the driver. An example of a "zoom" web for a project on "homes" is shown in Appendix 7.

A second technique for narrowing or broadening the focus of a topic is in terms of specificity or generality. Related topics can be located in a hierarchical classification, from the more specific to the more general. The more specific a topic, the more likely it is to be suitable for a project with younger children. Similarly, topics are likely to be more suitable for younger children if explored in a project spanning a shorter time. Examples of hierarchically related topics that are different in scope are as follows:

1. hats, uniforms, clothes
2. tortoises, reptiles, wild animals
3. my bedroom, my house, my village
4. weather, seasons, climate

The choice of project title as a focus for the work need not be limiting, however. In the case of the weather, no matter how young the children, the work can be extended to include the seasons or the climate. These more remote, abstract concepts would most likely not be developed in such detail by the younger ones as by older children.

A third way of narrowing the scope of a topic, especially for children in the preschool period, is to predicate it in some way, as Blank (1985) suggests. Blank argues that the predication of a concept is vital to any dialogue about it. It is difficult to have a conversation about food, for example, until the term is predicated in some way that gives it a particular contextual meaning. Once it is known whether one is thinking about buying food, serving food, or preparing food, the word *food* takes on a significance that can generate conversation. Giving alternative perspectives to the topic of houses can indicate a direction for study: "building a house," "houses in our neighborhood," or "furnishing a house." A project about shops may have subthemes such as "going shopping," "shops in our Main Street," or "setting up a shop."

Predicates can be particularly useful in reflecting the children's interests and ideas on a main topic. The three techniques discussed here for narrowing the scope of a topic for a project with younger children or for completing it in a shorter time have been found useful by teachers in adapting topics for particular groups of children.

If a school or a class has problems arranging visits outside the school, many projects within the school can give the children direct firsthand experience and topics that they can pursue for several days. On a walk around the school grounds, objects such as rocks, grasses, twigs, leaves, and seeds can be collected. These can then be examined closely in the classroom. They can be drawn, labeled, sorted, and looked up in books. Such a project is described in Appendix 8, "A Walk Around the School" (Chard, 1971).

Teachers can also capitalize on young children's tendencies to become collectors. For instance, when the children have been alerted to the interesting variety of seedpods freely available in their environment, they can start a collection in the classroom. Each child can bring in new examples every day to be studied in relation to others along several dimensions (see Appendix 2 for guidelines).

FIVE PLANNING CRITERIA

In chapter 4 we discussed *relevance* as the principal criterion for selecting project topics. Five other criteria for selecting and focusing particular project topics should also be considered: the activities that the children can undertake, applying skills, the availability of resources, the interest of the teacher, and the time of the school year.

Activities for the Children

No matter what the topic, certain kinds of worthwhile knowledge, skills, dispositions, and feelings are developed through project work. Although groups of children may undertake projects on different topics, much similar learning will take place. Whether the children study "birds feeding," "vehicles for cargo," or "clothes for cold weather," each topic offers opportunities for close observation, labeling of parts, counting and tallying (counting in groups), making bar charts, sorting according to different criteria, finding and recording information from books, negotiating with other children, and collaborating in group activities. The activities give children the occasion to observe, to reconstruct aspects of the environment, and to practice finding things out. These skills and processes are being learned and practiced with every project undertaken, although the prominence given to particular skills and processes may vary from one topic another.

Some topics are particularly rich in potential for investigative activities, while others offer more opportunities for dramatic play. In their planning, teachers are generally concerned with achieving a long-term balance in the kinds of opportunities that the project is likely to provide for the children.

During initial planning, the teacher develops a web to which the children's own ideas can be added. A familiar hospital in the neighborhood can be an important focal point in the web and project plans. Some of the children may have been to the hospital themselves or had relatives there. It is likely that they and their siblings were born in the hospital. Some of the parents may work there. If so, one part of the web may be developed more fully to include resources well known to the children.

Understanding hospitals might best be achieved by asking children to explore the common experiences they have had with local doctors. These experiences vary in different parts of the world. Children in rural areas of China are likely to be familiar with the barefoot doctor, her role in the community, and the instruments she uses. Children in rural India will probably be familiar with the primary health center in their community and its procedures and services. Many children in the Australian outback will have experience with visits of the flying doctor. Whatever the location, the doctor or district nurse might be willing to visit the school to talk to the children. Each culture offers different perspectives on the topic, and these can be reflected in the activities of the children as they develop the project.

Applying Skills

Project work gives children the opportunity to apply skills independently for purposes that they themselves have generated or helped to formulate. These purposes will arise from the children's own experience. Even within one class, children show different levels of competence and confidence in a variety of basic skills. Most children apply skills independently only when they feel confident and comfortable enough in the setting. They do so especially if the aim of the activities is learning rather than performance (see chapter 2, p. 36).

The level of competence at which a child uses a skill unaided is not always related to the level of competence displayed during instruction or assessment. A quite able child may be reluctant, for example, to use a reference book to find out how water comes out of a bathroom faucet, whereas a much less able child may be eager to seek such challenge (Dweck, 1987, 1988). In other words, just because a child has a competence does not mean he or she will use it. Children may be reluctant to look things up because their reading experiences have typically been with basal readers or reading schemes (Br.).

Other important factors besides competence contribute to children's behavior. Feelings of self-efficacy, confidence, degree of interest based on prior knowledge or experience, learning style, and other individual attributes play a role in this variability of response to the challenge involved in applying skills independently.

Sometimes confident children, highly motivated to obtain information from a reference book, will persist with reading the material even though much of it is too difficult for them. Similarly, in adult life some people may choose at times to attempt difficult tasks that stretch them almost beyond the limits of their ability. At other times they may confidently prefer to work with more risk-taking and originality at something that is easy for them. So too in project work, children can choose from a variety of levels of challenge. This is another example of the way project work can bring activities in school closer to the quality of real-life experience, a major theme of the project approach. Projects offer the teacher opportunities to encourage children to work at an optimum level of confidence and to select different levels of challenge.

When children work independently, they might be expected to take more time at their tasks, to take risks, to be more exploratory and imaginative in their thinking than under conditions of direct instruction. For example, preschool children can learn about the purposes of reading and writing before they can actually read or write. In their play they can make shopping lists, "write" prescriptions, or follow recipes. Play or pretend writing may take the form of scribbling even after children are receiving writing instruction, just as there is a short overlap between a baby's crawling and walking when both methods of locomotion are practiced alternately. When writing comes to children easily, they use it with fluency and have no need for scribbling, just as infants drop the crawling when they become confident walkers.

The application of language skills is an important concern in teacher planning. Project work provides rich content for conversation not only on the topic itself, but also on the range of processes involved in the work. Children use language purposefully as they involve themselves in the activities. Project work offers children shared experiences of events to think about and discuss with one another. The experiences gained while working together on various aspects of the project become integrated with current understandings as children talk in a variety of situations.

The dramatic play area (home corner, domestic play space) can be equipped with props that stimulate conversation in role playing. When children not only dress up in nurses' and doctors' uniforms, but also have stethoscope, syringes (with needles removed, of course), thermometer, a sling, bandages, a blood pressure gauge, and empty medicine bottles, their play becomes considerably more focused on specific information. They can think about the diagnosis and treatment of illness and what medical personnel can do to help. Thus many aspects of language development are stimulated and strengthened.

Language is the principal means by which young children can share, negotiate, and even create meaning. In the process of planning, the teacher can assess the potential of the project for adding to the children's growing store of words, expressions, and phrases. Children not only have to acquire new vocabulary. They also have to learn ways of using the words in scripts or basic sequences of related events leading to predictable outcomes in particular contexts and for particular purposes (see the discussion of event and script knowledge in chapter 2, p. 23).

While selecting and planning a suitable project, teachers can list the language associated with different understandings. For example, *diagnosis* involves finding out what is wrong with a patient, where it hurts, how much it hurts, how hot she is, how long she has been ill. *Treatment*, on the other hand, refers to what must be done to help the person feel better and recover from the illness or injury. The two concepts, diagnosis and treatment, are distinct; though similar vocabulary is used, diagnosis and treatment are associated with different goals.

During planning, teachers can take into account the ways that children use their behavioral knowledge in developing their representational knowledge. When visiting the doctor, children may exhibit the behavioral knowledge of being a patient: showing their tongue, coughing on request, and later taking medicine. The project activities help children develop representational knowledge that distinguishes behaviors related to diagnosis from those concerned with treatment.

Various cognitive processes are involved in the development of representational knowledge. Children actively engage in comparing and contrasting objects and events, note attributes of things, take them apart and reassemble them, group objects into classes, order them, and string them together in scripts. Hohmann, Banet, and Weikart (1983) offer a useful selection of "key experiences for cognitive development," tested and applied in the High/Scope curriculum for young children. Another useful set of aims for conceptual development, particularly in science, can be found in the Schools Council $^{15}/_{13}$ Project, *With Objectives in Mind* (1972, pp.60–65).

Appropriate communicative skills can be developed as children work cooperatively, questioning, speculating, reasoning, inferring, and explaining their project-related work and actions. For the youngest children in the age range of concern here, communicative competence can be strengthened when they are encouraged to ask each other's advice, tell each other what they are planning to do, and ask each other questions about their work and progress in the project.

The basic academic skills of reading, writing, and mathematics can be employed when school-age children record observations, describe experiences, and note down what they have found out in books. Some projects offer greater opportunities than other projects for applying certain basic skills. In a store project with older children, there might be more opportunities for particular mathematical skills to be applied; in a study of the neighborhood, map-reading and other graphic skills can be used. Most projects provide many varied opportunities for using skills in drawing, talking, writing, reading, mathematics, and science.

Availability of Resources

The term *resources* is used very broadly here to include any sources of information and experience such as field trips and classroom visitors, as well as material resources that contribute to the activities and learning of the children. The resources available for the children's work and play are a major consideration for the teacher when planning a project.

If, for example, the teacher introduces a project on "going to hospital," she might ask herself the following questions about resources: Where might the children visit (local clinic, doctor's office)? Who might be invited to talk to them in school (nurse, doctor)? Might this visitor have some discarded instruments, some old X-ray pictures to donate to the project? What resources does the school have from previous hospital projects (doctors' and nurses' coats and uniforms, charts, books)?

Teachers experienced in using the project approach often accumulate a personal collection of potentially useful items. In addition, parents may be requested to contribute to the school's collection by donating equipment and other items to exhibit, to work with, or to enrich play, for example, bandages, crutches, and empty medicine bottles.

Sources of information, experience, and resources can also be found beyond the school walls: the public library, local museum, businesses, factories, and educational resource centers. For example, children growing up in fishing village can gain much knowledge from a project on "How we get our fish," as shown in the web in Appendix 9. There is also a particular value in the children collecting resources from home, being given or loaned items, and collecting some on a visit they themselves have made. This initiative further illustrates the principle that young children's learning is maximized through effective interaction with their environment and the people in it.

In particular, projects should be planned so that they include a significant proportion of firsthand and direct experience of real objects and people. The proportion of such experiences should be high in relation to secondhand information gained from books and visits to museums where the information has already been experienced and presented by someone else. If the project topic is about the neighborhood, local industry, or the natural environment, then resources may be plentiful and easy to obtain. Parents can be involved in the project, talking to the children about some special expertise, helping with field trips, and lending or giving objects, pictures, photographs, or other resources to the classroom.

If the topic is distant in time (e.g., Victorian England or castles) or in space (e.g., Japan or animals in the polar regions), the children will have only secondhand and indirect information and will thus be very dependent on the teacher for their learning. Projects of this type provide little or no personal experience and firsthand information on which children can base their contributions to the work of the project.

When children are older (from eight to twelve years), they have enough general knowledge and awareness of learning strategies to learn a great deal from secondary sources. From eight years on up, children can infer much information that is analogous to their own direct experience. They also share a set of public concepts that approximate or overlap those of the adult culture.

For young children, however, the availability of a store of general knowledge cannot be relied upon, because their knowledge of the larger world is still being formed. When, for example, nine-year-olds study the Nile, some general knowledge about a local river can be relied upon. But young children acquire general knowledge about rivers most easily through studying a nearby river, one whose bridges they cross with their parents, or fish in, or walk beside. The teacher can share the children's experience of the river on a field trip and gain a fuller insight into their interests and understanding.

Teacher Interest

It is also helpful if the teacher chooses a topic in which she herself has some personal interest and basic knowledge. In project work the teach-

er is an important model to the children. She exemplifies the dispositions she wishes to strengthen by helping children with their explorations, encouraging and acknowledging questions, discussing, and
demonstrating an inquiring disposition. To do so, she uses books, pictures, charts, maps, and so forth to find out where the children can look
for appropriate information.

Because the range of topics is wide, teachers need not repeat the
same projects every year or even every three or four years. Each year
they can usually plan some projects that are new, fresh, and personally
challenging to the teacher as well as to the children. However, since the
children have an important influence on the way projects develop, a
responsive teacher seldom finds that even a repeated project takes the
same course with a different class group.

Time of Year

When the teacher first becomes acquainted with a new class of children, it is helpful to choose a topic that they have experienced personally and are ready to share with others. For example, families, babies, or
homes are topics that are very much a part of their everyday lives. The
openness that can be fostered at the beginning of the academic year is
well worth developing early, because it facilitates the teacher's understanding of individual children. Understanding is important for building relationships that help the children feel secure and through which
they can be helped to explore their classroom environment with confidence.

VISITS TO PLACES OF INTEREST

Some advanced planning is desirable if it is appropriate to arrange a
field trip to a place of interest, a walk around the school neighborhood,
to a local store, or to farm. It is usually a good idea for the teacher to
visit a site before taking the children to it. Information obtained by
phone or letter rarely provides enough detail to serve as a basis for
preparing the children for a productive class visit. When the teacher
makes an initial visit, she is likely to see points of interest in all kinds
of unanticipated places. Consider, for example, visiting a park to gain
firsthand appreciation of the opportunities it offers to people living in
the neighborhood. In addition to what the teacher already knows about
the park, a preliminary visit may yield useful information related to the
interests of her own class. For instance, one group of children will
appreciate the patterns in the wrought-iron gate at the entrance to the
park; another group might prefer to read the signs on the trees and

walls; and one or two individuals may want to spend most of the time studying the birds on the pond.

The staff of a department store, railway station, or clinic may find it difficult to visualize in advance the invasion of twenty young children. The teacher can help allay their anxiety and promote their understanding of what she hopes the children will gain from the experience. When a visitor comes to talk to the children in school, it may also be important for the teacher to explain in advance what she expects the children to gain and what they will be like. When given the opportunity to question a policeman who had finished speaking, one young child felt compelled to tell the man about his aunty's parrot that had just died, not quite appreciating the role of the police in relation such small-scale disasters.

SUMMARY

Throughout the period of initial planning, teachers find it useful to identify the key events that might occur in the life of the project, for example, a visit, a speaker, displays, central activities to be undertaken by individuals or groups, products of the work undertaken, and a culminating event to draw the work to a close. These events are described in some detail in chapters 6, 7, and 8. Once the preliminary planning has been undertaken, teachers can implement the project during the phase we call "Getting Projects Started: Phase I."

CHAPTER 6

Getting Projects Started: Phase I

Some projects claim the children's interest from the first minutes; others require more effort from the teacher. Not all children will be equally interested in all topics. However, the way the teacher introduces the project can be an important factor. In this chapter we discuss various ways of engaging children's interest when launching a project. We begin by considering ways of involving children during the preliminary discussions in the earliest stages. Next we describe types of activities that are particularly appropriate for getting projects started. These are followed by suggestions for involving parents.

ENGAGING CHILDREN'S INTEREST

Children's attention is easily captured by the novel and the unexpected. This is especially true when they can relate the novel to something they already know. A brick, some mortar, a detached faucet, or a doorknob can raise interest immediately, because they look strange when detached from the houses children live in. Similarly, objects that children may have seen only at a distance, for instance, a wheelbarrow, a bicycle, or a sewing machine, can offer much to observe and talk about. Entirely new objects such as an oar from a rowboat, a beehive, a blood pressure gauge are also fascinating. The culture of the classroom where projects are undertaken encourages children to be curious about new things or familiar objects in new contexts.

Pictures provide a good stimulus for interest, especially if they are related to the objects presented. For instance, items of house construction might be accompanied by pictures of builders, plumbers, or electricians at work. The medical equipment might be shown in a picture-story sequence of a sick child going to hospital for treatment and getting well again. A brief slide show can also be a good introductory stimulus, especially if there are plenty of opportunities to follow up on children's questions afterwards.

When the project follows other projects, the children can be reminded of relevant events and experiences that had been particularly enjoyable. They might look forward to similar occasions in connection with the new project. The sense of a common group history strengthens the sense of community, and the teacher can do much to encourage this in simple, incidental ways. For example, a study of the neighborhood may include a walk around the streets close to the school. The teacher might remind the children how interesting they had found their walk to the supermarket earlier in the year during the project on buying food.

INTRODUCTORY DISCUSSION

The initial discussion should make a strong impression on the children. It is a good idea to present something arresting, engaging, arousing their curiosity, and inviting interest. The teacher might tell a story, and one or more objects might be displayed or passed around. Open discussion about the topic reveals the degree of familiarity the children already have with the topic. Their views and comments about particular items are welcomed.

In the early class discussions, teachers will find it useful to let children recount events in their own experience of the topic. For instance, in a hospital project many of the children will be able to talk about their own accidents that resulted in a visit to the hospital. The discussions will generate script knowledge, knowledge about sequences of events leading to a goal, which many children will use spontaneously in their dramatic play. Children can also be encouraged to talk about their play and their use of the equipment. As they articulate their need for some new prop such as a stethoscope, the teacher can encourage and help them to design and make one or acquire a real one.

At the beginning of a new project, the children's enthusiasm is easily aroused. It is therefore important that excitement be kept at an optimum level to avoid setting expectations that might not be met. Undertaking a project is a serious matter, and steady application on the children's part is required to achieve much of the work planned. In this initial discussion, the children should be invited to think about the project. Over the following few days, they can suggest work they would like to undertake and aspects of the topic they want to explore and learn more about. The teacher and children can think of items they might collect from home to display on walls and horizontal surfaces.

During the early discussions, the teacher finds out the language and behavioral knowledge at the children's disposal for talking about relevant experiences. She learns what children can already say about the topic and where they might have difficulty. Sometimes clear misunderstandings and conflicting impressions are exposed, leading to animated exchanges among the children. The teacher should not be too ready to correct children in the group situation, since this may inhibit participation in the discussion. Instead, the teacher's approach at this point might be to draw their attention to the opportunities they will have to find out more and to clarify their understandings.

During the initial discussions, the teacher can suggest activities, some of them to be undertaken by individuals and others by small groups working together. Suitable activities are discussed below.

ACTIVITIES FOR EARLY STAGES OF EXTENDED PROJECTS

When a project with older children is planned to last for several weeks, there is time to allow for qualitative change in the activities as the work develops. At the beginning, however, relatively unstructured activities are most helpful to the teacher in assessing the children's prior understanding. Dramatic play, painting, drawing, and writing from memory about personal experiences related to the topic are suggested activities. Each of these is discussed in turn below.

Dramatic Play

If the classroom does not have a play area, it would be a good idea to start one. A square of inexpensive carpet or matting can be laid in a corner of the room to delimit a small area. A three-sided screen with a door in one side and a window in another can also be placed there (Figure 6). Because it is flexible, this basic arrangement can become a farmhouse, a hospital, a hot-air-balloon basket, a camper, or a boat. The teacher and children can discuss how to prepare the play area for a suitable topic related to dramatic play. The children are likely to be very interested in the transformation of the area from one project to the next.

For the present discussion, the theatrical term *props* is used to refer to objects that the teacher introduces to enrich dramatic play. Dramatic play is particularly enhanced if the children have real objects as props. The children's understanding of events is reflected in the way they use the objects that are part of those events. Props also enable the children to replay the sequence of events that takes place in the real world, for example, to role-play the scripts related to hospital events, a store, or a

Figure 6. Room arrangement options.

home. Usually at the beginning, few unfamiliar props should be contributed for play because the children should have familiar things they associate with the specific topic. As project work progresses, less familiar objects can be added.

To illustrate the points made above, let us look at the hospital project. The play area can become a hospital with a row of dolls in cribs, a child-sized cot, a chair, dresser, and a sink. Props can include plastic medicine bottles, an arm sling, and bandages. It is a good idea to add steadily to the props throughout the life of the project. Later additions may include X-ray pictures displayed against a window, a thermometer, patient charts, stopwatch, and various doctor's instruments. The quality of the play changes across the three phases of the project, and the functions fulfilled by the props become increasingly useful in refining and elaborating children's understanding.

From observations of children at play, the teacher can identify understandings and misunderstandings. The following examples of misunderstandings have been reported: "The doctor makes you better when he puts the thermometer in your mouth" and "I'm going to be a doctor when I grow up, because then I'll never get ill." Such revelations can provide information that can be used to clarify understandings in later group discussion.

Children have to accept certain conventions or precautionary rules about not putting things in their mouths, not using large instruments near their faces, having no more than six children playing in the hospital at one time, and the like. Such rules are usually readily accepted when the reasons for the precautions are given. Some rules can be generated by the children themselves to solve problems that emerge during their play.

Drawing, Painting, and Writing

Because various kinds of art work and writing are important ways of communicating understandings, teachers can encourage children to apply these skills in project work. The effectiveness of communication can best be judged in relation to the people to whom the message is addressed. Project work can offer opportunities for children to communicate with the whole group, the teacher, parents, and children in other classes.

Bulletin boards can be used to reflect different aspects of the project so that the children can see their own work. The teacher can ask the children to suggest where and how their work should be displayed. She can also use many opportunities to draw children's attention to items on display. She can ensure that some aspects of the display change frequently so that the children continue to notice what is there.

Children can work individually or collaboratively. For example, a group might construct a "wall story," which is an illustrated sequence of events depicted in paintings and writing. The story might be about a child who has an accident and goes to hospital for treatment. This is another representation of a script. It can be displayed near the play area so that the children can refer to it in their role play. For example, a dispute about the order of events arose among some children playing in the class hospital. Together they consulted the events depicted in the wall story to settle the dispute.

Children will be able to draw and paint pictures of the events they remember from their own experience of illness or accident. In one class, the teacher found that all of the children had a story of some sort to tell about how they had hurt themselves. She suggested that they write and draw their stories and collect them in a book called "Accident Stories." In this way, children can read about the real things that have happened to them.

PARENTAL INVOLVEMENT

Parents can be involved in project work in at least four ways. First, parents and children can easily share information about projects, because the topics are likely to be familiar to them. For instance, children can ask their parents whether they have been to hospital or ask to see where the hot water is heated. Children and their parents can be encouraged to communicate about the real world. Some teachers particularly welcome the opportunity to speak to parents as a group about their intentions for children's project work during the year. In this way, they can prepare the parents for the children's requests for information and other contributions to the project.

Second, parents can be encouraged to ask their children how the project is progressing and what activities they are undertaking. Often parents find it difficult to obtain intelligible replies to questions about what their children are doing in school, especially in some areas of the curriculum. In project work, however, the teacher can help the children talk about their work at home by suggesting events and aspects of the work to discuss with their parents. In so doing, the teacher establishes communication and accountability with the parents. Communication gives the children an additional opportunity to practice the new language they are learning in school. Parents also learn about aspects of the curriculum associated with the application of skills and the development of dispositions that are likely to help the child succeed in school. Certain skills and dispositions in particular are generally less well understood and appreciated, for example, the dispositions to persist in the face of difficulty and to vary the problem-solving strategies when first attempts fail.

Third, the parents can be very helpful in providing information, pictures, books, and objects to help the whole class in its pursuit of knowledge on the topic. Sometimes a parent who is a doctor or a nurse is willing to talk to the children during a health-care project. A father who is a mail carrier may come and talk about his work and bring some items from the post office. Parents can assist in arranging a visit to a factory, a farm, or a store. As part of project work, the children can write letters home, asking for specific information such as common childhood diseases they have had and at what ages. For a project on babies, the children may find out when they cut their first teeth or learned to walk unaided.

Fourth, at a later stage of the project, parents might be invited to come and see the work the children have been doing. Each child can guide his or her parents around the display areas, and the class can sing a song or put on a small play they have written. Such visits help parents gain confidence in the school and in their own contribution to the child's continuing informal education at home. Parents can thus feel involved in an important part of their children's schooling.

SUMMARY

Observation of children at play and at work can inform the teacher of understandings and misunderstandings. She can also learn about the children's preoccupations or concerns, such as mothers going into hospital to have babies. Sometimes children play out anxieties that can be shared and alleviated. Children may also develop interests in some part of the topic through their play. An interest in the heart or bones can be followed up by reference to books, observations of a lamb's heart, pictures, X-rays, and so forth.

Towards the end of the first phase and the beginning of the second, the teacher can look back at her web plan of the project and evaluate different parts of it in light of what she has learned about the children so far. By the end of the first phase, a field trip will have been arranged or maybe a visitor planned. The teacher then begins to prepare the children for this event by talking with them about the kinds of things they can expect to see and learn.

CHAPTER 7

Projects in Progress: Phase II

In this chapter we discuss ways of maximizing children's interest through group discussion, offering new experiences, encouraging them in a variety of activities, and reflecting their own progress back to them as the project develops. A selection of activities that children can undertake in pursuit of a fuller understanding of the topic is discussed, together with opportunities to practice skills and encourage desirable dispositions. The products of children's work are discussed and how they can be used to reflect learning and stimulate further questions. We also suggest ways the teacher might extend the challenges for more able children and structure special opportunities for children with learning or motivational difficulties.

CHILDREN'S INTEREST

One of the hallmarks of a successful project is the children's interest in it. However, teachers who have not used the project approach before should not be too easily discouraged if some children's interest appears to flag disappointingly soon. Children may lose interest in the project for many different reasons. They may not be learning anything new; their play may have become repetitive; they may be dissatisfied with their own contributions to the class work or feel unable to interest others in their ideas; they may sense that their parents take little interest in the project; or they may lack confidence in their own abilities in relation to the demands of the work.

Some projects simply do not seem to capture the children's interest as well as others. It is unlikely that all children will be equally interested in all topics. A teacher should ensure that at least one topic of real interest to every child in the class has been included among the topics undertaken over a period of a year.

Because many factors affect a project, its success cannot always be predicted beforehand. If the children lose interest in the main project but wish to investigate a related area, it is wise for the teacher to follow their lead rather than try to stay too rigidly with the first ideas. However, the teacher is very influential and can do much to ensure that interest is sustained.

Children vary in the extent to which they become interested in projects. Some children are interested in every project, some show little interest in any school activity, and others are interested in some things but not in others. In this chapter, we suggest many ways to revitalize and maintain interest in the projects. Children are responsive to variety, fresh and direct experience, and opportunities to share their concerns with others. Projects offer the teacher opportunities to respond to the wants and preferences of individuals while showing them the contribution they can make to the work of the whole class.

In this second phase of the project, the teacher may organize focal events such as a field trip or a classroom visitor. These events can provide important sources of questions, information, and ideas of interest to the children. Group discussions are a valuable way to prepare children for a new experience and to debrief them afterwards by helping them to share their understandings of new information.

GROUP DISCUSSIONS

Discussions with the whole class or with smaller groups have both informative and motivational functions. At the beginning of the project, discussions enable the children to share what they as individuals know about the topic, and they enable the teacher to explore the children's present understandings. In the second phase, discussions have several additional functions: to prepare the children for a field trip, a class visitor, or other focal event; to help children formulate questions for investigations; to plan group learning activities; to evaluate what has been accomplished; to talk about the work being undertaken; and to plan future work. In discussions, the teacher helps children share the thoughts and experiences they are having, thus promoting the community ethos in which the work will thrive as she sets expectations and directs activities.

Young children's discussions should have interesting and mind-engaging content. When they feel involved with the content, there is less need to repeat the rules of hand raising, turn taking, and attending. Children will listen to others because they want to hear what is being said. The teacher's talk can consist of comments as well as questions (chapter 2), and children can be encouraged to interact with each other so that not all of the conversation directly involves the teacher. In this way, she can provide a model of an interested listener for the children. Her comments on the children's talk also model appropriate replies and reflections on what another person says in a conversation.

FIELD TRIPS

Young children collectively can be interested in almost every imaginable aspect of a trip outside the school. Few details escape their notice if the teacher, together with the children, has made clear the expectations for the main purpose of the trip. The teacher can encourage awareness of the more routine aspects of the visit such as arrangements for transport, meals, and groupings of children with particular adults. These routine aspects give the children practice in classifying, counting, and representing pictorially and symbolically the events of the day.

For example, older children can write descriptively in the following manner: "There were twenty-seven children and five adults on our bus. This was thirty-two people from our school and thirty-three people altogether with the driver. The bus had forty seats for passengers, so eight seats were empty." Inevitably the children will be interested in the mode of transport and the food, and these interests can provide useful opportunities for teaching and learning. The teacher of course can also draw the children's attention to features of the trip that are pertinent to the main work of the project. The younger children can dictate their impressions for the teacher to record.

Some teachers find it useful to have the older children take notebooks or clipboards for making notes and sketching interesting items they see. Usually it is preferable to leave such on-the-spot recording open-ended. When the teacher supplies a checklist of items to look for or a list of questions to answer, children can be distracted by the "treasure hunt" quality in these activities. Instead, if she suggests only a few things to look for, the children can observe them closely and with interest rather than vie with each other to discover items on a common list.

Younger children's attention can be drawn to people or objects, their functions, how they work, and how they relate to other objects or people. The grouping of objects on the basis of common characteristics and their differentiation from other kinds of objects require children to observe closely. Analytical discussion is encouraged, and later on in the classroom the teacher can help the children represent their observations in various ways in pictures, charts, and writing.

Consider, for instance, a visit to a clinic. The children are likely to see a thermometer, blood pressure gauge, and stethoscope, all of which are instruments for diagnosing what is wrong with a sick person. The children are also likely to see surgical scissors, a hypodermic syringe, and forceps, which are used to treat a person once the problem is diagnosed. After the visit, a discussion can lead to the distinction between the two sets of instruments. The children's understandings of the two sets and how they overlap can be represented pictorially in a Venn diagram of two overlapping sets (Figure 7). The inclusive class of objects is labeled "instruments," and the distinction between the subsets is based on the difference between the functions of diagnosis and treatment. A small flashlight might be used for both. Children's labeled drawings can be grouped appropriately in the diagram, which can be

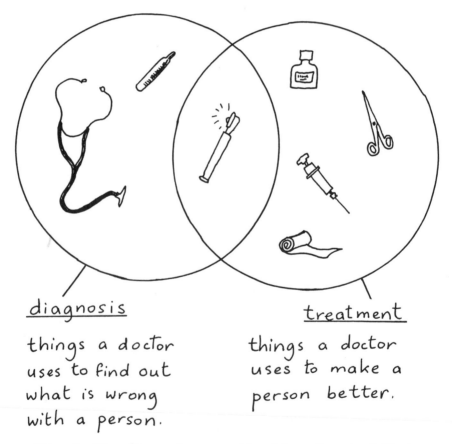

diagnosis

things a doctor
uses to find out
what is wrong
with a person.

treatment

things a doctor
uses to make a
person better.

Figure 7.   Venn diagram to represent two intersecting sets of objects.

displayed with a child's written commentary about the information summarized in the diagram. Other children might write questions that can be answered by referring to the diagram: "Which instrument is used for both diagnosis and treatment?" "Which is the smallest instrument used for treatment?" or "Which instruments made of glass are used in diagnosis?"

If a museum is being visited, the children may be able to separate into groups, each with a particular interest to follow. Each group of maybe four or five children should be supervised by an adult who need not be a teacher. Parent volunteers can be briefed by the teacher to encourage observation and recording and to talk with the children about what they are seeing. Back at school, each group can report what they saw and noted. When children share with others who did not see the same things, there is a clear purpose to their communication, and the other children can be encouraged to ask questions to clarify their understanding.

Using illustrated books, the children can elaborate on their own sketches and fill out descriptions. More questions can be asked and answers sought. Often new information leads children to ask more questions in school after the visit. If the museum is a local one, some children who visit it regularly with their families may be willing to make a weekend trip there to gather additional information needed. Otherwise, the children can write to the museum after a visit to clarify points that may arise back in the classroom.

Interest is strengthened when the topic is treated in the kind of depth made possible by direct experience of real-world settings. For instance, the mathematical skills of comparing, sorting, classifying, and ordering, which are often acquired and practiced in artificial and disembedded settings, can be applied to project work when the children study an item of real interest to them. Studying the parts of an ambulance, for instance, may lead to a comparison of the materials in it: metal, plastic, wood, and fabric. The substances that make the engine work—gas (petrol, Br.), oil, water, and air—can be compared in various ways according to their function.

If the teacher cannot take the children outside the school to visit an appropriate site, an expert may be invited to visit and bring objects or pictures to leave on loan to the class. Sometimes when it is impossible to go outside the school for direct firsthand experience, something can be arranged within the school building or on school grounds. In the walk around the school described in Appendix 8, children can study the items they collect on their way. Another alternative is to ask the school janitor to accompany the children on a tour of the school, showing them where the materials and equipment used to clean and maintain the building are kept. They might then make a plan of the school building. If school meals are cooked on the premises, the children can see what is involved and observe the people who do the work. Above all, the point of a field trip is firsthand experience. If it can be provided any other way, it can compensate for not going out on a visit.

ACTIVITIES FOR LEARNING

As the project progresses, children can undertake a wide variety of activities, which are discussed here under three headings: construction, investigation, and dramatic play. We also discuss various ways that children can apply the basic academic skills of language (talking, reading, and writing), mathematics, and science to each of these types of activity.

Construction Activities

As children build models, they ask questions about design and construction. The models can be made of junk material, clay, and wood, as well as from construction toys, kits, or other materials. Children can talk about what to include in their model; for example, they can discuss the parts of the ambulance, both outside and inside. They can talk about the problems they are solving as they construct the model—how to fasten the wheels on, the scale of the model, and how to fit all of the necessary items inside. Finally, they can discuss the finishing touches such as the red cross and the lights to complete the model to their satisfaction.

Basic skills, language arts, and mathematics are applied in activities related to the construction. These activities are enriched when the children can read about the ambulance, for instance, in books and study detailed pictures of it and its functioning. The writing of older children about the object they are constructing may be of two kinds. First, they can report how they made the model and describe the materials, strategies, and techniques that failed and succeeded. This writing might be collected in a class book about model construction or displayed alongside the model itself. Second, the children can write about events involving their ambulance: a journey to pick up a sick person in an emergency, an accident, or the life and work of an ambulance driver. This writing might form part of a display showing different aspects of the work of the hospital.

In mathematics, many activities related to the construction of the ambulance can be undertaken. Parts have to be measured to fit together, and relationships of width, length, and height can be considered. Some mathematical understanding can add depth to the construction of the dashboard with its dials and gauges.

Investigation Activities

The primary purpose of investigation activities is to find out information. After being introduced to the topic, children who have gained confidence in what they already know about it can be encouraged to go further, to find out new information, to build on their basic understandings. New places and objects can be explored, and questions can be asked. The teacher can help extend the children's repertoire of active investigation strategies. In the classroom, children can hypothesize, estimate, and experiment. For example, in a study of the manufacture of clothing, children can find out about different fabrics by designing a test to compare fabrics for insulation or waterproofing efficiency. They can try to simulate some of the processes involved in producing fabric for clothing by growing, collecting, and cleaning cotton, wool, or linen. They can try spinning, dyeing, or weaving yarn or thread to make cloth.

Receptive strategies that children can use to investigate a topic include observing, listening to an expert, watching someone at work, and reading. Observation involves looking closely at objects, handling them, and maybe using other senses. Instruments used by doctors, tools used by builders or plumbers, and equipment used by cooks can all be studied closely, and the cause-and-effect relations implicit in their use can be noted—for example, the shape of the parts of a stethoscope for picking up and transmitting sounds, a syringe for injecting, and a hospital bed with mattress, pillows, head-rest, and progress chart for accommodating a patient.

Observations can be set up over a period of time so that changes can be noted, measured, and recorded. Growing plants in the classroom offers such opportunities, as do studies of the weather, animals, and birds outside the classroom window. Recording observations in drawings, writing, and tallies enables children to reflect on the learning involved in the observation. This can be further represented in mappings, charts, and graphs.

Investigation can often be motivated by construction activities. The older the children, the greater their concern with realism in their constructions; for example, the relative height, width, and length of the ambulance being built may become significant.

Dramatic Play

Dramatic play can be stimulated after a field trip by adding new props such as x-ray photographs and patients' progress charts. New scripts can be learned, such as visiting a sick friend in hospital; going there to have a baby, an operation, or a broken bone set after an accident; and the roles of doctors and nurses in these scenarios. New understandings of the functions of objects and people are reflected, and new misunderstandings noticed and clarified.

Dramatic play in the second phase involves trying out new information in context. Children rehearse the new understandings embedded in situations that they can be helped to imagine through accounts and stories, thus making their own best sense of the topic. Role-playing activities can lead directly to questions. Children may want to know the journeys typically made by the ambulance in the area or in a given period of time. According to the age and understanding of the children, such investigation provides opportunities for work on direction, time, speed, and distance. In studying the work of the ambulance driver, the children might chart or map the places the driver goes in one day to pick people up or take them home or to another hospital. The ambulance driver may also have considerable training in first aid to offer emergency help such as giving oxygen or carefully positioning a person with a broken limb on the stretcher.

PRODUCTS OF WORK

The work that the children produce may include pictures, pieces of writing, charts, graphs, models, and board games. These products can be stored in personal folders or mounted in individual books. They can be displayed in a class book focusing on one aspect of the project. They can be displayed on vertical and horizontal surfaces such as walls, windows, tables, and shelves. Children's work displayed under sub-themes or particular aspects of the project serves various functions for the teacher and the individual child, as well as for the whole class.

The wide range of task complexity usually accompanying project work offers very able children an excellent opportunity to undertake challenging tasks suitable to their ability. Likewise, it offers an interesting selection of important but much simpler tasks to children who have learning difficulties. Teachers can help structure the tasks and advise individuals about how to apply their skills to maximum effect. This strategy is likely to strengthen children's motivation to collaborate with other children as they are able without fear of being shown less competent. The following example illustrates this point.

A small group of children were working together on a picture of an ambulance. They wanted to display it with strings running from different parts of the vehicle to word labels around the outside of the picture. Two children wrote the labels, one measured and cut suitable lengths of string, and the third pinned the strings in place. The child who pinned the strings would have had great difficulty writing the labels, but his contribution was valued because he performed a necessary task. At the same time, he improved his reading ability while matching the words and objects.

CLASSROOM DISPLAYS

Display areas devoted to the project can be major focal points for classroom-based activity as the work develops. During the first phase of the project, displays give children the opportunity to collect, sort, represent, and share current understandings of a limited range of relevant items. As the project progresses, the emphasis shifts to three other functions of display: (1) to provide information that children can refer to in their work and play, (2) to reflect children's growing experience of the project and show a developing record or diary of the work, and (3) to communicate the children's discoveries and achievements to particular audiences (their own teacher and classmates, other teachers and classes, the principal or head teacher, parents, or any other visitors to the school).

During the second phase of the project, these functions of display become still more important. Each function is discussed below.

Displays for Information

Displays are most informative when they include key words for children to use in their writing. In this way, they serve as a specialized glossary or word book. The children can compile an alphabetical list for reference, in addition to the easy-to-see labels of objects on display (all letters in lower case for young children). Pictures, photographs, reference books, maps, charts, and a small selection of commercially produced material can be displayed for information. Children's own pictures and writing can also be informative, as well as imaginative or reflective. Various pictorial and symbolic representations are undertaken specifically to present discoveries in an organized form that enables easy retrieval of facts by other children needing the information. Bar graphs can present frequency information. Venn diagrams provide a mapping of information in sets of objects that have some similarity or are parts of wholes. The same set of objects that are parts of a thing can be classified into subsets according to different attributes. For instance, an ambulance has parts made of metal, rubber, glass, wood, plastic, and fabric. These same parts can be classified differently according to whether they are part of the transport function of the ambulance or the health emergency function of it. As the children gain experience in analyzing items in project work, they are more likely to suggest ways of their own for presenting information to others. When tasks differ from child to child, achievements should be shared so that the new understandings can benefit other members of the group. An informative display is particularly interesting when it depicts things that the onlookers have not personally experienced, but that they can easily assimilate in terms of what they already know.

Displays as a Record

The second function of displays during the second and third phases of the project is to provide a record of the life of the work as it develops. The contributions of individual children and cooperating groups provide a growing source of information about the achievement of the class. The teacher uses this record to reflect back to the children the progress they are making in their investigations. The children become familiar with the displays and take pride in their own and each other's work. In doing so, they are motivated to assimilate the new information where it enriches what they already know. They are also motivated to rework and accommodate their understanding to information that conflicts with their earlier concepts.

The shared and public meaning of things is given due status by display. The evidence of the children's work around the classroom is formally useful throughout the life of the project as a record of the achievement of the class for the teacher, the principal or head teacher, the parents, and other interested parties.

Displays to Communicate to Outsiders

The third function of displays is to offer children a place to communicate what they would like to tell others about their work. This function overlaps with the record-keeping function. It is, however, different in a very fundamental way. When displays are used as a record, some of the charts and observations children make are part of their investigation of an object or event. In contrast, when displays are intended for others, children sometimes write a description of their own work and what it adds to their personal understanding of the topic. They can write for children in another class, for older or younger children. They may develop a quiz or a series of questions that can be answered by referring to a graph or to a mapping of groups of items.

To return to the ambulance example, a quiz for older children might include this question: "What is the largest thing that is made of rubber and is part of the health emergency function of the ambulance?" And for younger children: "What is the smallest metal instrument used by the doctor in finding out what is wrong with the patient?"

One of the best ways a person can be sure of understanding something is to try explaining it to someone else. When explaining things, we have to put ourselves in the mind of the other person and predict what we will need to say or write to ensure understanding (Benware & Deci, 1984). Children can write captions for graphs and diagrams that explain to other children how to extract information, or they can write or dictate to the teacher instructions for games. Children can design and make simple board games for two players on some aspect of a project.

For the hospital project, they might design a dice and track game where some of the squares or positions on the track represent getting sick or having an accident, while other squares represent possible remedies or help from medical personnel. Setbacks for patients can be indicated by the instruction to "miss a turn" and positive gains by the instruction to "take another turn." On a different topic, one group of children explained their playground games in writing so that others who had never played these games could learn by following the rules. Another group tried them out and offered ideas for improving the instructions.

THE TEACHER'S ROLE

The scene is set for the project during the first phase, when the teacher evaluates the children's levels of understanding and interest in the project. In the second phase, the class revises and enriches their understandings on the basis of firsthand experience through visiting an appropriate location, looking closely at objects, discussing real events, and talking with people who are involved with the setting being studied. The teacher orchestrates the learning events, shaping the overall outcome of the project. Some of the activities the children can be engaged in are painstaking and slow-moving, others spontaneous and short-lived. Some play is open and free, other activity highly structured and focused.

In this second phase, the teacher is strengthening the children's dispositions to be resourceful, independent, imaginative, involved, cooperative, and productive. The timing of when to provide resources is related to activities the children can undertake, where possible optimizing interest. Timing is important in maintaining the momentum and depth of the work. The following is an example of judicious timing in a study of two tortoises.

During the project's first phase, lasting one week, the children observed and recorded the physical parts and attributes, activity, food intake, and behavior of one female tortoise. In the second phase, lasting two weeks, a male tortoise was introduced. The children then made a comparison study of the two animals, reviewing their understandings of the female and comparing in detail the female with the male. Thus the study had two purposes: (1) finding out about one tortoise and (2) comparing two tortoises. Had the teacher introduced the two tortoises at the same time, the amount of interest would have been halved, since activities that were repeated with a new purpose would have been undertaken only once with both purposes lumped together. Repetition is a valuable way of learning, but its efficiency may be reduced by boredom when an experience is presented in the form of practice tasks.

We do not wish to suggest that the activities described in this chapter usually happen spontaneously in work on projects. They do not. However, the teacher can use many ways to help children pursue construction, investigation, and dramatic play. Children can be encouraged to ask questions and think about the possibility of alternative answers. They can be helped to see how observation can lead to questions, which in turn can lead to experiments. They can be taught how records of observations can be translated into reports of discovered information. Children can gain personal satisfaction from increasing their competence. They can appreciate the products of their efforts as these contribute to a record of the learning of the whole class. The teacher is instrumental in promoting the classroom ethos, which enables children to cooperate, appreciate one another, and share the work of their class with others.

Compared with work produced through systematic instruction, the standards, complexity, length, level of difficulty, and precision in project work tend to vary considerably among the children's achievements, because the children do not always work to the limits of their ability. Some will be free-wheeling, while others will be working at a level far beyond their customary performance, owing to some special interest in the activity. The teacher can be instrumental in ensuring that the more mature and more able children are sufficiently challenged by their work. She can also find many opportunities to motivate less able children in the varied classroom context that the project approach affords. Standards may vary among the different pieces of work produced by any one individual on the same project. The teacher notes these differences and monitors the general performance of individual children over time.

Although the teacher continues to have an active role in the second phase of the project, the orchestration of learning consists in her being responsive to children as they attempt to solve problems and to master tasks. They need encouragement when their confidence weakens, suggestions when they run out of ideas, answers to their questions, direction to other sources of information, or new objects to boost their interest. The excitement that accompanies the initial stages of the project should be replaced by a sustained interest and satisfaction in the work being accomplished.

SUMMARY

The second phase of a project is concerned mainly with providing children new firsthand experience and helping them think about it in many interesting ways that stimulate purposeful activity and involve the use of various skills.

In this phase of project work, the children are learning to monitor and evaluate their own efforts and achievements. They are also being taught to respond to their own view of themselves, to trust their own judgment, to identify their uncertainties, to pose their own questions, and to risk trying when success is uncertain. The principle involved here is that children should be encouraged to rely on the database of their own personal experience. It is also important that the teacher encourage the children to share and appreciate the good work being done and to be helpful to one another in setting and achieving appropriate and satisfying standards. Children can learn to ask each other for advice, to discuss strategies, and to consult as they work together.

CHAPTER 8

Consolidating Projects: Phase III

Sooner or later projects in the classroom have to be concluded, even though children should recognize that learning on any topic is never really finished: there is always more to learn. A topic is merely set aside until the next time it is encountered, either within or outside the school context. Various approaches to concluding a project are discussed in this chapter.

Where preschoolers are involved, the decision to end a project can be made by the teacher in consultation with the children. The teacher takes into account play around the project constructions and materials. If frequency and quality of play have declined to a low level, she may ask the children whether they are ready to dismantle the project or set it aside in some special way. Similarly, if the play ceases to change, develop, or be elaborated after a week or two, the teacher can discuss with the children their readiness to end the project. If no new props are added or if constructions are not extended after a week or two, the children may have exploited the topic as much as they want to at that particular time.

The teacher may then suggest that the children contribute pictures or dictated stories for a class book about their work. If the project included a large construction, the children may be interested in organizing guided tours to explain their project to children in other classes. When the time comes to end the project, it is a good idea for the children to take responsibility for dismantling it themselves, preserving some elements and saving materials that can be used for subsequent projects.

Three aspects of the concluding phase of a project with older children are discussed in this chapter. First, children can usually gain a sense of closure if the teacher and the whole class together develop a shared view of what they have learned and achieved during the project. This can be done by arranging one or more culminating activities such as giving a presentation to other classes, to the whole school, or to parents invited in to see the work.

Second, the children should not become bored with the topic. Interest in the activities should be sustained, and everyone should remain at least somewhat involved in project activities until a new project is embarked on. Many interesting ways can be used to encourage children to elaborate and consolidate their newly acquired understandings.

Third, children should reflect on the work they have been doing individually and as a group so as to appreciate their own growing competence. The teacher can help them evaluate the work accomplished. An awareness of their corporate learning can help children value the collaboration involved in so many of their activities. Individuals can take stock of what they have learned about their own learning. They have new strategies and skills, as well as new confidence to bring to the next topic. The teacher's role is crucial in setting the tone during the final weeks or days of work on a project.

During the first and second phases of a project with older children, much of the work should address the realities of the topic. The work should include observations, descriptions, experiments, and problem solving. The boundaries between the real and the imaginary, the probable and the fantastic can be clarified in the course of working on a project.

Once the children are familiar with the main aspects of the topic, they are prepared to invent, create, and imagine characters and places for stories to write or plays to act. During the third and final phase of a project, activities that enable children to consolidate their understanding, applying newly acquired information in imaginary contexts, are appropriate. When these activities lose their appeal, the children are probably ready to move on to the next project.

CULMINATION OF A PROJECT

Activities undertaken during the second phase of a project can generate interesting and informative products. As these accumulate in individual project folders, in class books, and on wall displays, they constitute a rich resource that serves as a communal record of the project's progress since its beginning. A different story can be told about each project. No two classes of children will ever develop quite the same ideas and interests, undertake the same tasks, or solve the same problems. The uniqueness of each project reflects the distinctive thinking of each class of children and their teacher. A school assembly, an open house, or an invitation to parents and administrators to visit the classroom offers the teacher and children the opportunity to give an account or tell the story of the project to interested outsiders. The displays show achievements of the children, and each child can talk about his or her own work and the work of others.

PRESENTATIONS TO OTHER CLASSES

Where the whole school meets in daily assemblies, one day a week is often set aside for individual classes to talk to the other children and the teachers about their work (a common practice in Britain). Very large schools are sometimes divided for such gatherings. In some schools, meetings are held once a week so that the same kind of sharing can take place. Sometimes a class can talk to just one other class about its work. Such communications enhance the children's feelings of belonging to a larger social unit within their school. The spirit of caring about the learning throughout the school community helps to create an ethos in which the older and the younger children respect and support each other inside and outside the classrooms. The older children first listen to the achievements and efforts of the younger children and then present what they have been working on in a way that the younger children find interesting.

Some of the larger pieces of work such as paintings, charts, and models can be shown at these meetings. Selected children can describe how these items were made and what they represent. Individuals might read a description, story, or a poem they have written. A small group might put on a brief play while the rest of the class acts as chorus, singing or playing incidental music on percussion instruments. Or the whole class might sing or play music together. The teacher can coordinate the presentation of these products of project work, narrating the story from both the children's point of view and her own. Preparing for a presentation is usually enjoyable and energizing for the children and offers opportunities to summarize formally the highlights of the project for individuals and groups. Class discussion takes on a reflective and summarizing function, helping the children to appreciate their own and others' achievements.

We want to stress that a presentation is primarily a communication rather than a performance. A presentation offers the children the opportunity to represent and share their experience with interested others, and it offers the other children, teachers, and parents the opportunity to hear about the experience. Entertainment is not the main purpose, although these occasions often have entertaining features. The event is intended to communicate learning, but it does not need to be a precisely learned, formally scripted and rehearsed occasion. Room can be allowed for spontaneity and improvisation. If children are accustomed to this kind of experience from an early age, most of them will not be overawed by an audience. The emphasis here, as in other aspects of project work, is on engaging children's minds in the processes of learning. Children talk as much about the activity and how they worked as they do about the products of their work.

These learning processes involve making models, writing stories, designing and conducting experiments, recording observations, representing information in graphs, and so forth. The emphasis is not primarily on the product, although the product is important as a record of the process. Children can learn to explain, describe, report, and record the way they worked. For example, if two previous versions of a drawing were instrumental in achieving quality in a third and final version, the child can report how she or he modified the drawing in each successive effort. First drafts are not described as "mistakes" or as evidence of "where I went wrong," but rather in terms of "when I realized" or "when I saw how I could do it differently" to achieve a desired effect. Children who describe their efforts in terms of trying out alternatives before attaining the most satisfying outcome are communicating the value of such an approach. They model an awareness of learning strategy for other children and show how their thoughtfulness contributed to the final work. Project work can thus strengthen dispositions to persist in the face of challenges and to strive toward mastery and learning.

OPEN HOUSE

Another form of a culminating activity is an open day or open house when the class can report on the project to parents, administrators, or other visitors. Children can give visitors a personal guided tour of the classroom, or they can make a more formal presentation along the lines described for the school meeting. It is a good idea to give parents the opportunity to see how their responses to the request of the teacher and their child have contributed to the project. If parents have been very involved, the visit will be especially interesting to them; if they have not been, it may suggest ways they can help in the future and may encourage them to do so the next time.

SUSTAINING INTEREST

A major strength of the project approach lies in helping children connect new learning with their previous experience. Connectedness implies that new information can pervade and affect much of children's current understanding about other experiences and aspects of their lives. Children benefit from opportunities to think about new information in the context of their past experience. These opportunities also enable the new ideas to influence a range of current understandings. When new knowledge is internalized in this way, it is less likely to be forgotten. In the third phase of a project, the teacher can suggest many interesting activities that help children to consolidate their understanding.

CONSOLIDATION ACTIVITIES

The process of consolidation involves applying the knowledge acquired in familiar situations to a range of other understandings. To illustrate the activities that facilitate this process, let us take a close look at a project on the weather. New knowledge is likely to have given children the sense that the weather is less arbitrary than they had previously believed. They may have come to understand better that many everyday happenings are directly related to the weather—clothing they wear, the washing being quickly taken off the clothes line, gardening tasks, roof repairs before winter, the timing of a visit to the shops. Young children observe their parents doing many things for no apparent reason. Often adults do not make their reasons explicit even when questioned.

Consider the example of taking the laundry inside before a storm. A father rushes out to collect the clothes that are not quite dry. His four-year-old child, standing somewhat in the way, asks, "Daddy, why are you doing that?" The father might give one of several possible answers: "The washing will get wet." "Mind, out of the way, I have to do this quickly!" "It's going to rain any minute!" "Look at those dark clouds over there!" "Your mother is upstairs!" "Get your tricycle in before it rains!" A one-sentence answer to a child's question about an event presupposes that the child has the background understanding necessary to make sense of the answer (even if it is not a non sequitur). The child might be left wondering, "What has the rain to do with the washing?" or "Why doesn't mother come down and do it?" and so on. In their dramatic play and through writing poems, stories, or captions for paintings, children can give reasonable explanations for familiar events in the light of their new knowledge about how the weather affects our lives.

Sometimes consolidation activities allow children to elaborate peripheral interests in the project. In the school bus project, for example, older children might draw a map of an imaginary town with its school and children's homes. They might set and solve problems about the "best" routes a bus might take, given the location of the school and the homes. Not all of the ideas will come from the teacher. The children may have many ideas themselves. The displays remain a source of information, and various tasks connected with them can still be undertaken. Where appropriate, information on display can be used in connection with tasks that test children's understanding. The displays at this stage may be polished for public view during an open house. Most of the work products in the third phase can contribute to the children's own personal project folders, which form the records of individual progress.

EVALUATING THE PROJECT

At the conclusion of any project, it is useful for the children and the teacher to reflect on the skills, techniques, strategies, and processes of exploration that the children have used in the project work. All of these competencies can be applied with greater proficiency and confidence in a project on a new topic.

Much evaluation can occur when planning a culminating presentation, for instance, when the teacher and class discuss the various special events or group and individual achievements. If each of the children has been keeping work in a project book or folder and the teacher has been monitoring their progress, she will know which children require help to complete work and which would benefit from supplementary activities to clarify limited or erroneous understanding. Some teachers also find it helpful to encourage children to look back at their own work during the course of the project.

Information on the bulletin boards can be used during this phase as a basis for formulating and responding to quiz questions. These can be a practical method of checking on the new knowledge that individual children have learned.

Children can also talk with each other and the teacher, either in a class group or individually, about the skills they have practiced in the project. The teacher can help to summarize these skills to ensure that they are more easily available when the children embark on the next project. For instance, if the children have counted frequencies for a survey, they may have tried alternative ways of recording items and counting them in groups or tallying them. They may have compared the efficiency of chunking the items in twos, threes, or fives. Discoveries about the most efficient way to count and record the results can be influential in similar situations in the next project. The skills can be practiced in subsequent surveys. The older the children, the more explicitly these evaluations can be discussed.

Teachers' records of individual progress throughout the project will vary in specificity according to the age of the children. With the youngest children, few if any records will be kept. With school-age children, some schools require more extensive records than others. In school systems that require detailed records of children's progress, the teacher can list all of the activities undertaken by each individual, some of the groups, or the whole class.

For each child, a record can be developed that notes which activities were undertaken and the level of proficiency. One approach is to compile a matrix with curriculum competencies on one axis and the main project work activities on the other. When a competency is used in a particular activity, a check mark can be entered in the appropriate cell in the matrix. In this way, the project activities can be mapped onto the competencies. As each child works on an activity, the appropriate check on the matrix can be circled. Thus the competencies practiced can easily be seen. A recording method designed by Fay Moore is shown in Appendix 10. Keeping precise records of achievement is more complex with project work than with work sheets and standard test. Nevertheless, teachers should not be discouraged from incorporating the project approach into their curriculum.

In addition, records of what the whole class accomplished in the project can be useful for future reference. The web that was devised in the initial planning stages can provide a framework for this record. Using different colored markers or some other method of marking, the teacher can note the activities accomplished, the visits made, the resources used, and the areas most fully investigated. She may also want to note aspects of the project that were of lesser account or that remained unexplored. Activities or events that occurred but were not in the original plan can be added to the diagram.

An anecdotal account of how the web was expanded can serve as an additional evaluation of the project. A record of the whole project from the teacher's point of view is useful if she should wish to repeat a similar project and could be of interest to other teachers undertaking project work in a similar area. In some schools, records of this kind are kept on file as a planning resource. In this way, teachers can share ideas and make their experience available to each other.

WHERE NEXT?

As the work of a project draws to a close, the teacher sometimes recognizes a strong new interest emerging. In the bus project, the children's dramatic play might have led to play about the bus taking them on holiday. They might have considered what it would be like to go to different places, and they might have talked about where they had been and where they were likely to go later on. If this would be an appropriate project to do next, then the teacher might encourage the idea. The children might set up a travel agency, collect brochures, and make tickets to sell. The school bus construction, if not too dilapidated by this time, might be repainted as a tour bus, a ferryboat, or an airplane.

Or consider the school bus project of older children. Initially they might have focused on the bus itself, making models, experimenting with wheels and motion, and graphing the time required by different children to ride to school. They might have become interested in the various routes. This interest might then lead appropriately into a project on making maps of the neighborhood, thereby extending the children's graphic skills and increasing their knowledge of their larger environment.

Sometimes the teacher has an idea about which area of the curriculum she wants to emphasize in the next project. If so, she can try sowing the seeds of new interests as she sees their potential for future project work.

SUMMARY

The purposeful application of skills in project work opens up many possibilities for children. The classroom offers more interesting activities than any one child can ever do. Children learn to be selective in pursuing their own intentions in an environment where learning opportunities abound. With the teacher's help, they learn to make responsible choices based on interest. The third phase of a project is a time for elaborating new knowledge introduced in the second phase. It is a time to reflect on and evaluate what has been learned. It is also a time to look forward to new ideas and to the application of skills in the study of a new topic.

At the end of the school year, the teacher and children together can recall the more memorable events in the projects undertaken and reflect on the greater facility the children have acquired during that long period. In one school the teacher and children made a class book at the end of the reception (Br.) or prekindergarten year. The book included examples of individuals' work when they first started school. The children wrote about their early memories of school life and drew pictures of the events described. Each child could see how his or her own drawing and writing skills had advanced during the year. Through such activities, the children can become more fully aware of their increased competence and can be helped to look forward with confidence to the challenges in the year ahead.

CHAPTER 9

The Project Approach in Perspective

The project approach is not the sole answer to the challenge of engaging the minds of young children. But it is a promising means of stimulating dispositions that will endure for a lifetime. Because this approach to learning is so flexible, our introduction to it is intended merely as a guide. We know of no single orthodox way to implement project work.

Only some of the topics that might be of interest and value to young children are presented in this book. By definition, the project approach can encompass a wide range of topics that are locally relevant and culturally suitable to the participants. One of the challenges of incorporating projects into the curriculum is to identify topics that are appropriate for each group of children and features that are unique to their environment.

We see the project approach as complementary and supplementary to other aspects of the curriculum for young children. Early childhood educators and parents are not faced with choosing *either* free play or work sheets, for neither type of activity by itself sufficiently challenges young minds. Nor do we suggest that all conventional activities commonly provided for children be set aside. Some time should be allowed for spontaneous play. Many young children will also need carefully implemented, individual, systematic instruction to ease their way into complex basic skills. But we see nothing to recommend frivolous, fanciful, or mindless activities to the early childhood curriculum.

Webb (1974) points out that education must address two types of aims: instrumental and intrinsic. *Instrumental* aims assume that children are an "instrument" of society and that schooling is "an 'instrument' for purposes outside the school," such as preparing children for future occupations and other utilitarian and technical objectives. *Intrinsic* aims deal with those learnings that benefit children themselves. These aims include valuing knowledge for its own sake, aesthetic awareness, appreciation and sensibilities, and confidence in one's own questions. To these aims we would also add the dispositions to be experimental, reflective, analytical, and critical when confronted with a range of problems and issues. Clearly, all schools are obliged to address both the instrumental and intrinsic aims of education. In our view, the project approach allows both kinds of aims to be addressed equally well.

In chapter 2 we presented the case for project work, using research evidence to support our position. Abundant evidence can certainly be marshaled to support other views. A curriculum that directly instructs children in the skills usually assessed on standardized achievement tests clearly has an edge in producing the kind of success such tests indicate. But perhaps it is time to go back to the proverbial drawing board and develop methods for assessing certain other educational practices. We need to assess, for example, practices that help develop desirable dispositions such as children's eagerness to work and study without rewards, their level of interest in their projects, their willingness to come to school, and their general cooperativeness, peer interactive competence, and basic skills.

Early childhood educators have traditionally assigned great importance to the development of social competence (Biber, 1984; Isaacs, 1933). Recent insights into this aspect of children's growth confirm the wisdom of this tradition. Furthermore, recent research suggests that the groundwork for mature social competence is laid down in the early years. Virtually everything of importance that adults have to do requires interpersonal competence. Indeed, the major problems we face locally and worldwide are not simply technological, scientific, mathematical, or logical ones; they are primarily problems of a social nature. The quest for solutions to these socially based problems will undoubtedly continue for decades to come—when today's children have become tomorrow's adults.

The project approach, as we see it, gives teachers the opportunity to attend equally to social and intellectual development. Decision makers who are intent upon school reform rarely hesitate to cry out that improvements in education are necessary to cope with the economic and technological exigencies of the future. Early experience in working cooperatively on mind-engaging tasks may also improve the chances of being able to cope with the complex social issues of today and tomorrow.

There is a certain irony reflected in programs developed for youngsters who are dropping out of school in ever-increasing numbers. These programs appear to be most successful when they offer studies of problems that are *interesting* to the former dropouts (see Lasley, 1987). Is it possible that the psychological, social, and financial costs of such programs could have been spared if the participants' earlier education had been designed to offer more interesting, mind-engaging topics? This hypothesis is supported by the extensive follow-up studies of the High/ Scope Foundation (Schweinart et al., 1986a) and by the analysis of longitudinal studies of social development (Parker & Asher, 1987).

To date, empirical evidence supporting our advocacy of the project approach is primarily indirect. We do not yet have systematic and controlled comparative studies of an empirical and longitudinal nature that provide compelling evidence to support our views. Until such evidence is available, we suggest that teachers themselves experiment with the project approach. We are eager to hear about these experiments. From them, we hope to learn more about providing the education that best serves the long-term developmental needs of young children.

REFERENCES

Ames, C., & Ames, R. (1984). Systems of student and teacher motivation: Toward a qualitative definition. *Journal of Educational Psychology, 76*(4), 535–556.

Asher, S. R., Renshaw, P. D., & Hymel, S. (1982). Peer relations and the development of social skills. In S. Moore & C. Cooper (Eds.), *The young child: Reviews of research* (Vol. 3). Washington, DC: National Association for the Education of Young Children.

Azmitia, M. (1988). Peer interaction and problem solving: When are two heads better than one? *Child Development, 59*(1), 87–96.

Belsky, J. (in press). The "effects" of infant day care reconsidered. *Early Childhood Research Quarterly.*

Bennett, N. (1976). *Teaching styles and pupil progress.* London: Open Books.

Bennett, N., Desforges, C., Cockburn, A., & Wilkinson, B. (1984). *The quality of pupil learning experiences.* Hillsdale, NJ: Erlbaum.

Benware, C. A., & Deci, E. L. (1984). Quality of learning with an active versus passive motivational set. *American Education Research Journal, 21*(4), 755–765.

Bereiter, C. (1986). Does direct instruction cause delinquency? *Early Childhood Research Quarterly, 1*(3), 289–292.

Biber, B. (1984). *Early education and psychological development.* New Haven, CT: Yale University Press.

Blank, M. (1985). Classroom discourse: The neglected topic of the topic. In M. M. Clark (Ed.), *Helping communication in early education. Education Review Occasional Publication,* No. 11, 13–20.

Blyth, J. (1984). *Place and time with children five to nine.* Kent, England: Croom Helm.

Blyth, W. A. L. (1984). *Development, experience and curriculum in primary education.* London: Croom Helm.

Boggiano, A. K., & Main, D. S. (1986). Enhancing children's interest in activities used as a reward: The bonus effect. *Journal of Personality and Social Psychology, 51*(6), 1116–1126.

Bredekamp, S. (1987). *Developmentally appropriate practice in early childhood programs serving children from birth through age 8.* Washington, DC: National Association for the Education of Young Children.

Bretherton, I. (Ed.) (1984). *Symbolic play: The development of social under-standing.* New York: Academic Press.

Brice-Heath, S. (1987). *The quest for uncertainty.* Paper presented at the annual conference of the American Educational Research Association, Washington, DC.

Bridges, D. (1981). Accountability, communication and control. In J. Elliott, D. Bridges, D. Ebbutt, R. Gibson, & J. Nicas (Eds.), *School accountability: The SSRC accountability project.* London: Grant McIntyre.

Brown, A., & Campione, J. (1984). Three faces of transfer. In M. E. Lamb, A. L. Brown, & B. Rogoff (Eds.), *Advances in developmental psychology* (Vol. 2, 143–192). Hillsdale, NJ: Erlbaum.

Bruner, J. (1980). *Under fives in Britain.* Ypsilanti, MI: High/Scope Foundation.

Bruner, J. (1985). Vygotsky: A historical and conceptual perspective. In J. V. Wertsch (Ed.), *Culture, communication, and cognition: Vygotskian perspectives.* New York: Cambridge University Press.

Burton, C. B. (1987). Problems in children's peer relations: A broadening perspective. In L. G. Katz (Ed.), *Current topics in early childhood education* (Vol. 7, pp. 59–84). Norwood, NJ: Ablex.

Buss, D. M., & Craik, K. H. (1983). The act frequency approach to personality. *Psychological Review, 90*(2), 105–126.

Carey, S. (1986). Cognitive science and science education. *American Psychologist, 41*(10), 1123–1130.

Carpenter, J. (1983). Activity structure and play: Implications for socialization. In M. B. Liss (Ed.), *Social and cognitive skills: Sex roles and children's play.* New York: Academic Press.

Central Advisory Council for Education. (1978). *Children and their primary schools* (Vols. 1–2). London: Her Majesty's Stationery Office.

Clark, M. M., & Wade, B. (1983). Early childhood education. *Educational Review, 35*(2): special issue 15.

Cohen, E. G. (1986). *Designing groupwork.* New York: Teachers College Press.

Consortium for Longitudinal Studies. (1983). *As the twig is bent.* Hillsdale, NJ: Erlbaum.

Dearden, R. F. (1983). *Theory and practice in education.* London: Routledge & Kegan Paul.

deCharms, R. (1983). Intrinsic motivation, peer tutoring, and cooperative learning: Practical maxims. In J. M. Levine & M. C. Wang (Eds.), *Teacher and student perceptions: Implications for learning* (pp. 391–398). Hillsdale, NJ: Erlbaum.

Deci, E. L., & Ryan, R. M. (1982). Curiosity and self-directed learning. In L. G. Katz (Ed.), *Current topics in early childhood education* (Vol. 4, pp. 71–86). Norwood, NJ: Ablex.

Deci, E. L., & Ryan, R. M. (1985). *Intrinsic motivation and self-determination in human behavior.* New York: Plenum Press.

Department of Education and Science. (1978). *Primary education in England: A survey by H M Inspectors of Schools.* London: Her Majesty's Stationery Office.

Donaldson, M. (1978). *Children's minds.* Glasgow: Fontana.

Donaldson, M. (1983). Children's reasoning. In M. Donaldson, R. Grieve, & C. Pratt (Eds.), *Early childhood development and education.* London: Guilford Press.

Durkin, D. (1980). Is kindergarten reading instruction really desirable? *Ferguson Lectures in Education.* Evanston, IL: National College of Education.

Dweck, C. S. (1986). Motivational processes affecting learning. *American Psychologist, 41*(10), 1040–1048.

Dweck, C. S. (1987, April). *Children's conceptions of intelligence.* Paper presented at the annual conference of the American Educational Research Association, Washington, DC.

Dweck, C. S., & Leggett, E. L. (1988). A social-cognitive approach to motivation and personality. *Psychological Review, 95*(2), 256–273.

Egan, K. (1985). Imagination and learning. *Teachers College Record, 87*(2), 155–166.

Elliott, J., Bridges, D., Ebbutt, D., Gibson, R., & Nias, J. (1981). *School accountability.* London: Grant McIntyre.

Entwisle, D. R., Alexander, K. L., Cadigan, D., & Pallas, A. M. (1987). Kindergarten experience: Cognitive effects or socialization? *American Educational Research Journal, 25*(3), 337–364.

Evans, E. (1975). *Contemporary influences in early childhood education* (2nd ed.). New York: Holt, Rinehart & Winston.

Fein, G., & Rivkin, M. (1986). *The young child at play: Reviews of research (Vol. 4).* Washington, DC: National Association for the Education of Young Children.

French, L. A. (1985). Real-world knowledge as the basis for social and cognitive development. In J. B. Pryor, & J. D. Day (Eds.), *The development of social cognition* (pp. 179–210). New York: Springer-Verlag.

Fry, P. S., & Addington, J. (1984). Comparison of social problem solving of children from open and traditional classrooms: A two-year longitudinal study. *Journal of Educational Psychology, 76*(1), 318–329.

Garvey, C. (1983). Some properties of social play. In M. Donaldson, R. Grieve, & C. Pratt (Eds.), *Early childhood development,* (pp. 11–24). Oxford, England: Basil Blackwell.

Gersten, R. (1986). Response to "Consequences of three preschool curriculum models through age 15." *Early Childhood Research Quarterly, 1*(3), 293–302.   -

Glaser, R. (1984). Education and thinking: The role of knowledge. *American Psychologist, 39*(2), 93–104.

Gottman, J. M. (1983). How children become friends. *Monographs of the Society for Research in Child Development 48*(3, Serial No. 201).

Greenberg, P. (1987). Lucy Sprague Mitchell: A major missing link between early childhood education in the 1980s and progressive education in the 1890s–1930s. *Young Children, 42*(5), 70–84.

Grolnick, W. S., & Ryan, R. M. (1987). Autonomy in children's learning: An experimental and individual difference investigation. *Journal of Personality and Social Psychology, 52*(5), 890–898.

Gross, N., Gianquinta, J. D., & Bernstein, M. (1975). Failure to implement a major organizational innovation. In J. V. Baldridge & T. E. Deal (Eds.), *Managing change in educational organizations: Sociological perspectives, strategies, and case studies* (pp. 409–426). Berkeley, CA: McCutchan.

Groves, M. M., Sawyers, J. K., & Moran, J. D. (1987). Reward and ideational fluency in preschool children. *Early Childhood Research Quarterly, 2*(4), 335–340.

Grusec, J. E., & Arnason, L. (1982). Considerations for others: Approaches to engaging altruism. In S. Moore & C. Cooper (Eds.), *The young child: Reviews of resarch* (Vol. 3, pp. 159–174). Washington, DC: National Association for the Education of Young Children.

Harrison, C. (1980). *Readability in the classroom* (pp. 33–50). Cambridge, England: Cambridge University Press.

Haskins, R. (1985). Public school aggression in children with varying day-care experiences. *Child Development, 56,* 689–703.

Hohmann, M., Banet, B., & Weikart, D. P. (1983). *Young children in action.* Ypsilanti, MI: High/Scope Foundation.

House, E. R. (1972). The dominion of economic accountability. *Educational Forum, 37.*

Howes, C., & Farver, J. (1987). Social pretend play in two-year-olds: Effects of age of partner. *Early Childhood Research Quarterly, 2*(4), 305–314.

Huckelsby, S. C. [S. C. Chard] (1971). *Opening up the classroom: A walk around the school.* Urbana, IL: ERIC Clearinghouse on Elementary and Early Childhood Education.

Hughes, M., & Grieve, R. (1983). On asking children bizarre questions. In M. Donaldson, R. Grieve, & C. Pratt (Eds.), *Early childhood development and education* (pp. 104–114). Oxford, England: Basic Blackwell.

Hunter, M., & Barker, G.. (1987, October). If at first . . .: Attribution theory in the classroom. *Educational Leadership,* pp. 50–53.

Isaacs, S. (1933). *Social development in young children.* London: Routledge.

Isaacs, S. (1966). *Intellectual growth in young children.* New York: Schocken Books.

Johnson, D. W., Johnson, R. T., Holubec, E. J., & Roy, P. (1984). *Circles of learning: Cooperation in the classroom.* Arlington, VA: Association for Supervision and Curriculum Development.

Johnson, R. T., & Johnson, D. W. (1985, July/August). Student–student interaction: Ignored but powerful. *Journal of Teacher Education,* pp. 22–26.

Kamii, C. (1985, September). Leading primary education toward excellence. *Young Children,* pp. 3–9.

Karmiloff-Smith, A. (1984). Children's problem solving. In M. Lamb, A. Brown, & B. Rogoff (Eds.), *Advances in developmental psychology* (Vol. 3, pp. 39–89). Hillsdale, NJ: Erlbaum.

Karnes, M. B., Schwedel, A. M., & Williams, M. B. (1983). A comparison of five approaches for educating young children from low-income homes. In Consortium for Longitudinal Studies (Ed.), *As the twig is bent . . . Lasting effects of preschool programs.* Hillsdale, NJ: Erlbaum.

Katz, L. G. (1977a). Early childhood programs and ideological disputes. In L. G. Katz (Ed.), *Talks with teachers* (pp. 69–78). Washington, DC: National Association for the Education of Young Children.

Katz, L. G. (1977b). Education or excitement. In L. G. Katz (Ed.), *Talks with teachers* (pp. 107–114). Washington, DC: National Association for the Education of Young Children.

Katz, L. G. (1984a). Contemporary perspectives on the roles of parents and teachers. In L. G. Katz (Ed.), *More talks with teachers* (pp. 1–26). Urbana, IL: ERIC Clearinghouse on Elementary and Early Childhood Education.

Katz, L. G. (1984b). The professional preschool teacher. In L. G. Katz (Ed.), *More talks with teachers* (pp. 27–44). Urbana, IL: ERIC Clearinghouse on Elementary and Early Childhood Education.

Katz, L. G. (1985). Dispositions in early childhood education. *ERIC/EECE Bulletin, 18*(2). Urbana, IL: ERIC Clearinghouse on Elementary and Early Childhood Education.

Katz, L. G. (1986). Current perspectives on child development. In L. G. Katz (Ed.), *Professionalism, development and dissemination: Three papers* (pp. 35–52). Urbana, IL: ERIC Clearinghouse on Elementary and Early Childhood Education.

Katz, L. G., & Raths, J. D. (1985). Dispositions as goals for teacher education. *Teaching and Teacher Education, 1*(4), 301–307.

Katz, L. G., Raths, J. D., & Torres, R. (1986). *A place called kindergarten.* Urbana, IL: ERIC Clearinghouse on Elementary and Early Childhood Education.

Kliebard, H. M. (1985). What happened to American schooling in the first part of the twentieth century? In E. Eisner (Ed.), *Learning and teaching the ways of knowing* (pp. 1–22). Eighty-fourth Yearbook of the National Society for the Study of Education, Part II. Chicago: University of Chicago Press.

Koester, L. S., & Farley, F. (1982). Psychophysical characteristics and school performance of children in open and traditional classrooms. *Journal of Educational Psychology, 74*(2), 254–263.

Krathwohl, D. (1985, March). Cooperative learning: A research success story. *Educational Researcher,* pp. 28–29.

Lasley, T. J. (1987, May). Teaching selflessness in a selfish society. *Phi Delta Kappan,* pp. 674–678.

Lepper, M. R. (1981). Intrinsic and extrinsic motivation in children: Detrimental effects of superfluous social controls. *Aspects of the development of competence: Minnesota Symposia on Child Psychology, 14,* 155–214.

Lougee, M. D. R., & Graziano, W. G. (n.d.). *Children's relationships with nonagemate peers.* Unpublished paper.

Maccoby, E. E. (1984). Socialization and developmental change. *Child Development, 55*(2), 317–328.

Maccoby, E. E., & Zellner, M. (1970). *Experiments in primary education: Aspects of project follow-through.* New York: Harcourt Brace.

McCracken, R. A. (1969). The informal reading inventory as a means of improving reading instruction. In T. C. Barrett (Ed.), *The Evaluation of chil-*

dren's reading achievement (Perspectives in Reading No. 8). Newark, DE: International Reading Association.

McCullers, J. C., Fabes, R. A., & Moran, J. D. (1987). Does intrinsic motivation theory explain the adverse effects of rewards on immediate task performance? *Journal of Personality and Social Psychology, 52*(5), 1027–1033.

Maehr, M. L. (1982). *Motivational factors in school achievement.* ED 227 095.

Medley, D. M. (1984). Teacher competency testing and the teacher educator. In L. G. Katz & J. D. Raths (Eds.), *Advances in teacher education* (Vol. 1, pp. 51–94). Norwood, NJ: Ablex.

Miller, L. B., & Bizzell, R. P. (1983). Long-term effects of four preschool programs: Sixth, seventh, and eighth grades. *Child Development, 54*(3), 727–741.

Morgan, M. (1984). Reward-induced decrements and increments in intrinsic motivation. *Review of Education Research, 54*(1), 5–30.

Mounts, N. S., & Roopnarine, J. (1987). Social-cognitive play patterns in same-age and mixed age preschool classrooms. *American Educational Research Journal, 24*(3), 463–476.

Nelson, K. (1985). *Making sense: The acquisition of shared meaning.* New York: Academic Press.

Nelson, K. (1986). *Event knowledge.* Hillsdale, NJ: Erlbaum.

Nelson, K., & Seidman, S. (1984). Playing with scripts. In I. Bretherton (Ed.), *Symbolic play: The development of social understanding.* New York: Academic Press.

Norman, D. A. (1978). *Note towards a complex theory of learning.* New York: Plenum.

Parker, J., & Asher, S. (1987). Peer relations and later personal adjustment: Are low-accepted children at risk? *Psychological Bulletin, 102*(3), 357–389.

Patterson, G. R. (1986). Performance models for antisocial boys. *American Psychologist, 41*(4), 432–444.

Pinard, A. (1986). 'Prise de conscience' and taking charge of one's own cognitive functioning. *Human Development, 29*(6), 341–354.

Plowden Committee Report. (1967). *Children and their primary schools* (Vol. 1). London: Her Majesty's Stationery Office.

Radke-Yarrow, M. (1987, April). *A developmental and contextual analysis of continuity.* Paper presented at the biennial conference of the Society for Research in Child Development, Baltimore, MD.

Rogoff, B. (1982). Integrating context and cognitive development. In M. E. Lamb, A. L. Brown, & B. Rogoff (Eds.), *Advances in developmental psychology* (Vol. 2, pp. 125–170). Hillsdale, NJ: Erlbaum.

Rosenfield, D., Folger, R., & Adelman, H. F. (1980). When rewards reflect competence: A qualification of the overjustification effect. *Journal of Personality and Social Psychology, 39*(3), 368–376.

Rosenshine, B. (1983). Teaching functions in instructional programs. *Elementary School Journal, 83*(4), 335–352.

Ryan, R. M., Connell, J. P., & Deci, E. L. (1985). A motivational analysis of self-determination and self-regulation in education. In C. Ames & R. E. Ames

(Eds.), *Research on motivation: The classroom milieu* (pp. 13–51). New York: Academic Press.

Schank, R. C., & Abelson, R. P. (1975). Scripts, plans and knowledge. *Proceedings of the Fourth International Joint Conference on Artificial Intelligence.* Tbilisi.

Schickedanz, J. A. (1985). *More than the ABC's.* Washington, DC: National Association for the Education of Young Children.

Schools Council. (1972). *With objectives in mind: Science 5/13.* London: Macdonald Educational.

Schwartz, S. L., & Robison, H. F.. (1982). *Designing curriculum for early childhood.* Boston: Allyn and Bacon.

Schweinhart, L. J., Weikart, D. P., & Larner, M. B. (1986a). Consequences of three preschool curriculum models through age 15. *Early Childhood Research Quarterly, 1*(1), 15–46.

Schweinhart, L. J., Weikart, D. P., & Larner, M. B. (1986b). Child-initiated activities in early childhood programs may help prevent delinquency. *Early Childhood Research Quarterly, 1*(3), 303–312.

Shepard, L. A., & Smith, M. L. (in press). Escalating academic demand in kindergarten: Some nonsolutions. *Elementary School Journal.*

Shuell, T. J. (1986). Cognitive conceptions of learning. *Review of Educational Research, 56*(4), 411–436.

Silberman, C. (1970). *Crisis in the classroom.* New York: Random House.

Slavin, R. E. (1983). *Cooperative learning.* New York: Longman.

Slavin, R. E. (1987a). A theory of school and classroom organization. *Educational Psychologist, 22*(2), 89–108.

Slavin, R. E. (1987b). Developmental and motivational perspectives on cooperative learning. *Child Development, 58*(5), 1161–1167.

Slavin, R. E. (1987c). *Grouping for instruction: Equity and effectiveness.* Baltimore, MD: Center for Research on Elementary and Middle Schools.

Spodek, B. (1987). *Knowledge and the kingergarten curriculum.* Paper presented at the annual conference of the American Educational Research Association, Washington, DC.

Stewart, J. (1986). *The making of the primary school.* Milton Keynes, England: Open University Press.

Taylor, J. (1983). *Organising and integrating the first school day.* London: Allen and Unwin.

Tudge, J. (1986). *Beyond conflict: The role of reasoning in collaborative problem solving.* Paper presented at the annual symposium of the Jean Piaget Society, Philadelphia, PA.

Van Ausdal, S. J. (1988). William Heard Kilpatrick: Philosopher and teacher. *Childhood Education, 68*(3), 164–168.

Walberg, H. (1984). Improving the productivity of America's schools. *Educational Leadership, 41*(8), 19–30.

Warring, D., Johnson, D. W., Maruyama, G., & Johnson, R. (1985). Impact of different types of cooperative learning on cross-ethnic and cross-sex relationships. *Journal of Educational Psychology, 77*(1), 53–59.

Webb, L. (1974). *Purpose and practice in nursery education.* Oxford: Basil Blackwell.

Wells, G. (1983). Talking with children: The complementary roles of parents and teachers. In M. Donaldson, R. Grieve, & C. Pratt (Eds.), *Early childhood development and education* (pp. 127–150). London: Guilford Press.

Wells, G. (1986). *The meaning makers: Children learning language and using language to learn.* Cambridge, England: Cambridge University Press.

Wertsch, J. W. (1985). *Vygotsky and the social formation of mind.* Cambridge, MA: Harvard University Press.

Willes, M. J. (1983). *Children into pupils.* London: Routledge & Kegan Paul.

Wisconsin Center for Educational Research. (1984, Summer). Ability grouping can hurt achievement. *News.* Madison, WI: Wisconsin Center for Education Research.

Wood, D., & Wood, H. (1983). Questioning the preschool child. *Educational Review, 35*(2), 148–162.

Yaeger, S., Johnson, D. W., & Johnson, R. T. (1985). Oral discussion group-to-individual transfer and achievement in cooperative learning groups. *Journal of Educational Psychology, 77*(1), 60–66.

Zimilies, H. (1987), The Bank Street approach. In J. L. Roopnarine & E. Johnson (Eds.), *Approaches to early childhood education* (pp. 163–178). Columbus, OH: Merrill Publishing.

APPENDIX 1

Houses: How Are They Built?

The web and journal excerpts that follow were adapted with the authors' permission from a project proposal written by Angela G. Andrews and Helen L. Hocking, kindergarten teachers at Scott School, Naperville, Illinois.

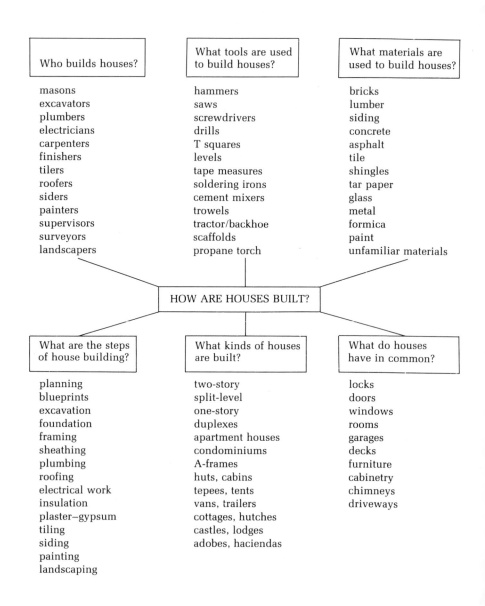

Who builds houses?	What tools are used to build houses?	What materials are used to build houses?
masons	hammers	bricks
excavators	saws	lumber
plumbers	screwdrivers	siding
electricians	drills	concrete
carpenters	T squares	asphalt
finishers	levels	tile
tilers	tape measures	shingles
roofers	soldering irons	tar paper
siders	cement mixers	glass
painters	trowels	metal
supervisors	tractor/backhoe	formica
surveyors	scaffolds	paint
landscapers	propane torch	unfamiliar materials

HOW ARE HOUSES BUILT?

What are the steps of house building?	What kinds of houses are built?	What do houses have in common?
planning	two-story	locks
blueprints	split-level	doors
excavation	one-story	windows
foundation	duplexes	rooms
framing	apartment houses	garages
sheathing	condominiums	decks
plumbing	A-frames	furniture
roofing	huts, cabins	cabinetry
electrical work	tepees, tents	chimneys
insulation	vans, trailers	driveways
plaster–gypsum	cottages, hutches	
tiling	castles, lodges	
siding	adobes, haciendas	
painting		
landscaping		

EXCERPTS FROM THE TEACHER'S HOUSE PROJECT JOURNAL

Visit #1

Today we visited the construction site. There are five houses, each one in a different stage of construction. One is just a hole in the ground, and one is a model home with a "For Sale" sign on it.

"Look at this big pile of dirt," said Tommy. "It's for the swimming pool," said Jimmy.

"It's a basement hole," corrected Michael. "We had one."

Some boys were looking at the sewer cover. "It says 'water' on it."

"I know about sewers. There's alligators down there," said Steven.

Some girls were wondering about the plastic on the outside. They couldn't figure out why it was there. "What color is this house gonna be?" they asked.

"Does this house say 'for sale'?" asked Justin. "I don't think so. There's no S on it," answered Heather.

Some men were carrying long pieces of board into the house. "Those boards are very longer," said Tommy.

A generator was running and there was lots of hammering noise and sawing noise. The children could identify these sounds.

Some men working on the roof waved to us. "Be careful!" yelled the girls. The men were listening to music and it was turned up loud. "They must like that station," the children agreed.

"I see some stairs in there," said Jessica. "We have some at home."

On the way back to the school, Michael pointed to the sign. "That says 'Hunter's Woods.' I see the H and the W." I asked why did the children think it was called that. "Maybe somebody used to hunt here a long ago time," guessed Erin. "A man named Mr. Hunter used to live here," stated Michael. I don't know if that is true but the children seemed to accept his answer as truth.

Visit #2

We went back to the house. The masons were putting a brick facade on one of the houses. One of the children asked them what the silver tanks in the garage were for. After telling them the reason, the worker invited us in. I hesitated only for a minute, thinking about liability [insurance] and safety, sized up the group and my control of it, and we went inside!

"There's going to be a basement!" said Steven.
"There's going to be an upstairs!" said Michael.
"I have tile like this on my floor," said Mary Ella.
"Where is the kitchen?" asked Tyler. The appliances and cabinets were not in yet.

"It's pretty big inside here," commented Jason.
"The lights will go in that hole up there—right?" said Meredith.
"That is called scaffolding," reported Mary Ella. "We had that in our house a lot."
"Look at all the doors in here. How many are there?" said Tyler. The doors were stored in the garage.
"We like your house!" the children yelled to the masons as we left.

Visit #3

On our third visit, the builder dropped by. We told him we were watching his house being built. He smiled and watched us for a while. We were very careful as we looked at the window wells.

(Back at school one of the boys went over to the [paper] cups, picked one up and looked at it a long time. "Can I cut this up for a window well?" I saw that the middle part is ridged very much like the wells [we saw on the houses being constructed]. Soon an assembly line of window-well cutters was begun. The class decided that only the cracked cups should be cut up.)

We see a pile of gravel by the foundation site. The second house has a new tar driveway and is roped off. The sidewalk is being completed near the third house.

Some boys wanted to know how the window wells are attached [to the building] and they spent a long time looking at this.

"There's a pole across today!" notices Michael as we approach the foundation. A builder nearby tells us it is an I-beam.

"What are these?" the children asked about the bolts protruding from the foundation. "That is how the decking will be attached," says the builder. Back at school the boys pour over my book that has a picture of this.

Visit #4

On our fourth visit, the children notice that the foundation has been sprayed black. I ask them why.

"Maybe they like that color," guess some of them.
"No. That's waterproof paint. It will keep the basement from leaking," states Michael.

A garbage truck drives up and takes away the scraps from in front of the house. The children watch this process but make no comment.

Visit #5

"There's a problem at the house. Want to go see what it is?" I ask on Monday. I have now got the habit of driving by and checking the house each day for signs of change. The children are eager to see.

"I told you it was a swimming pool!" said Jimmy. The basement is flooding. The children spot the problem. One of the pipes has burst. The basement is filling fast. "They need to cut off the water," says Justin, "or that basement is history!" (Justin loves to say things are history.)

The next day we went back to the site. A man was using a sump pump to get the water out. The pipe has been fixed. The water is going out into the street near a gutter. The children are fascinated by this sight. "How long will it take to get the water out of there?" asked the class. "I don't know," said the worker.

There is a lock on the door of the house we went in one day. "That's to keep the robbers out," said Evan. "No, we had a lock like that on my house. It means the house is for sale," said Erin.

We walk around the outside, counting the window wells. Later I see them doing the same thing with their models. "Oh, look—a deck is going to be here!" states Heather. "We have one of those."

Back at school, I noticed that children are building foundations with the blocks instead of their usual building [piling] up [blocks from the ground]. Matt wanted to draw plans for the foundation. He laid some paper on the floor and began to sketch it out. The other boys began to build on his plan. They roll their plans up and put them in the cubbies. I made a note to bring a tube to school and let them store them in there, the way my dad, an architect, used to store his plans.

Visit #6

"It's a blue house!" reported Erin. "I saw it on my way school."

Of course we have to go and see it. One of the houses has some blue siding on it now.

"I knew it would be blue," said Justin.

"Look at that hole in the side," points Shannon. "That's going to be a door." (It is for the fireplace.)

We notice that the driveway has been plowed up at one of the houses. We wonder why. "They just didn't do it right," says Michael.

Back at school I notice more evidence of carry-over. I overheard Tommy, who was drinking from a cup with a straw, say "That's how they got the water out" to no one in particular. I see that the boys are taping their plans together now.

"What can we use for the I-beam?" asks Nathan. They decide on a ruler. "We can use these for the joists," says Michael, indicating the unifix cubes. There is much measuring and comparing as they make the necessary boards.

APPENDIX 2

Guidelines for a Project on Seedpods

Particularly in tropical regions around the world, many varieties of trees, bushes, and plants bear their seeds in podlike structures (leguminosae). These pods can be collected as part of the children's school activities and after school hours. No field trips and special equipment are required.

Pods that individuals collect can be examined separately or pooled for sorting and examination in small or large groups. Some preliminary suggestions are listed below:

1. Identify the common and scientific names for the plants or trees the pods come from.
2. Sort and describe them by length: from shortest to longest; size: largest, smallest, widest, thinnest, thickest; and number of seeds in them. Measure actual length in inches or centimeters, and determine how many short pods equal one long pod.
3. Sort and describe by shape: flat, round, straight, curved, bulbous, tubular, cylindrical.
4. Sort and describe by color, hue, and luster.
5. Sort and describe by texture: smooth, rough, prickly, oily, ribbed.
6. Sort and compare by weight. Test to see how many small pods weight as much as a large one.
7. Describe by source: tree, bush, plant, flower.
8. Sort vegetable, fruit, and decorative pods.
9. Note whether they grow in clusters, groups, or singly, and whether they are symmetrical when opened. Note how the seeds are arranged inside the pod, whether it is transparent, and whether the number of seeds can be detected without opening the pod. Determine the largest and the smallest number of seeds found in each species, whether the seeds rattle when the pod is shaken, and how the pods change over time as the seasons change.

10.   Other activities: make musical instruments with the pods that rattle, draw and paint how favorite pods look on the plants.

11.   Drawing, painting, sketching, and tracing can be used to record observations, depending on the ages of the children.

APPENDIX 3

Dramatic Play in the Hospital

The following is a transcript of a recording of seven five-year-olds playing in the class hospital. The comments in brackets are those of Sylvia Chard, who observed the children.

Dr = doctor; N = nurse; V = visitor (mother of patient); P = patient.

[10:07 a.m. Children just settling, getting used to me. I bandaged a boy's finger on request, fearing that might have been the wrong thing to do, but he went away and busied himself very soon as Dr2.]

N1	Does she feel all right? Poor thing.
V	What room is she in?
Dr1	That's not how to do it.
N1	Lee, I do all the things.
P	I feel sick.
N1	Where's the medicine? I need some medicine.
N2	Give her some medicine.
Dr1	No you can't open that bottle. It's child proof.
N2	Where's that little white pot? Thank you.
N1	Go to sleep.
N2	She doesn't want to.

[Both nurses are being very attentive to the patient; one is sitting on the bed, on the patient, too.]

P	Why are you sitting on me?
N2	People have to sit on beds.

[10:12 a.m. Dr1 bandages patient's finger carefully, first with a tubular cotton-knit dressing, then with a gauze bandage, also using surgical scissors. N2 goes out of the room with a tray of cups. I later learned that she regularly takes a cup of tea to the teacher. N2 re-enters half a minute later with the tray of cups. Dr2 gives the patient medicine with a tin of Andrews Liver Salts and a plastic spoon. N1 telephones the patient's mother, V, who has gone out of the room to receive the call from home.]

N1	She's getting better now.
V	All right, I'll come.
Dr2	You'll like this, you've got to have this medicine today, it's nice, it's fizzy medicine.

[N3 has been spending most of the time so far arranging a variety of surgical instruments, medicine bottles, boxes, bandages, and cups and saucers on the shelves and in the cupboard at the side of the little room. Dr2 is mixing medicines in different jars from different bottles.]

Dr1	Here you are, this will make it better.

[He is sponging the patient's forehead very gently with a little white sponge, putting disinfectant on the sponge from a tiny bottle. The bottle is emptied and he says to the patient, "Here you are, you can keep it." Patient plays with the bottle. N3 is still arranging and rearranging items on the shelf.]

N1	(to patient) You're a teenager and you're having a baby. Now you've had your baby—she's broken her leg.

[10:17 a.m. She picks up a baby doll with a missing leg out of one of the three cribs in a row on the other side of the small room. Patient winces.]

N2	Go to sleep. I'll put your blankets on, or you might get a cold.
Dr1	She doesn't feel very well.
N1	She's having a baby.
Dr1	(trying to step out of the corner) Can I come out please?

[N2 talks sweetly with patient, covers her up, and kisses her good-night.]

Dr2	I've got some medicine to give her.
P	I want to kiss her (indicates V).
Dr2	I'm the doctor.
V	I'm her Mum.
Dr2	You're not allowed to . . . it's cough medicine to make the baby come out.

[After some moments of confusion, the patient becomes the baby and acts with much less restraint than hitherto; she cries, indicates she wants to get out of bed.]

N1	No you can't go out.
N2	Doctor, she wants you.
Dr2	This will keep her quiet.
Dr1	I'm back again.
V	Your doctor's here.
Dr1	You're not going to like this (gives her medicine). It's so we can give her an operation. So that's that done. I hope she doesn't wake up. (to patient) You're having your operation.
Dr2	(advancing with forceps) I'm going to take your heart out with these scissors.

[10:22 a.m.]

N1	And that'll make you stay asleep a long time.
N2	That's got her asleep!
Dr1	Look what's in her heart!
Dr2	Some brown stuff.
P	(wakes up expressively)
Dr1	(to nurse) Can you turn her face over please?
V	That's the new doctor you like.
Dr1	Can I have a look at your teeth? (pretends to probe in her mouth with instrument) I've got one of her teeth! It's got all blood over it.
N1	It's got all blood over it (echo).

[Patient tries to crawl out of bed and is put back by V and N2; Dr1 starts work at the foot of the bed.]

Dr2	I've got to check her hair (moves away).
N1	I'm checking her hair.
N2	The doctor's got to do that.
P	Ow, ow!
V	(to Dr1 who is working on the patient's foot) Stop it, Doctor, she's crying!
Dr1	I have to do it.
V	Stop crying . . . you can have a sugar lump if you be good girl!
Dr1	(businesslike) Right! That's it; finished.
N1	I'll get the injection.
P	Ow she's hurting me with her pin. . . .
V	(tickles patient) I'm making her laugh.

[10:27 a.m. Dr2 works with concentration, putting medicines together for several minutes.]

N2	Doctor, she won't. . . .
Dr1	Have your sugar lump. I can see your baby coming out . . . here's your baby . . . I'm going to have to pinch her baby out (waves his forceps).

Teach-
er: Could you finish your game and tidy up your hospital now? Babies need to be covered up; you must make them as comfortable as possible. Make sure all the medicines are on the shelf.

Child: She's bleeding!

Teach-
er: Make her as comfortable as possible. Put all the bandages in the box.

APPENDIX 4

Instructions for Children:
How to Make Your Own Book

HOW TO MAKE YOUR OWN BOOK

Planning

Decide   1. What is it about?
2. How big is it?
3. What shape is it?
4. How many pages does it have?

Work To Do on the Book

1. Think of a title.
2. Design the cover.
3. Do the writing (stories, poems, facts, or descriptions).
4. Draw the pictures.
5. Make any moving parts (fold-out or pop-up or pull-along).
6. Number the pages.
7. Write the table of contents (front).
8. Write the index (back).
9. Make any other additions you want (dedications, acknowledgments, "The End" page, decorations for first letters or words, patterns in page margins).
10. Don't forget the name of the author and the date you finish it.

APPENDIX 5

Project Webs for Going Shopping, Weather, and a Construction Site

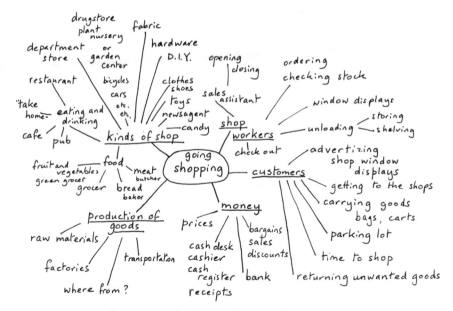

Shopping web designed by another teacher.

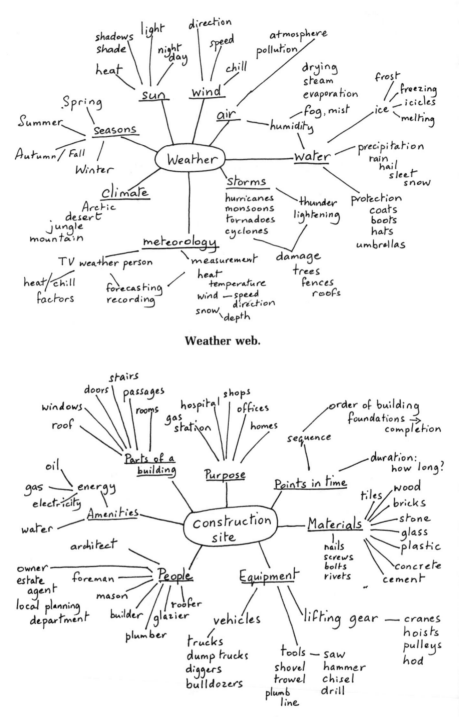

Weather web.

Construction site web.

APPENDIX 6

School Bus Webs for Younger and Older Children

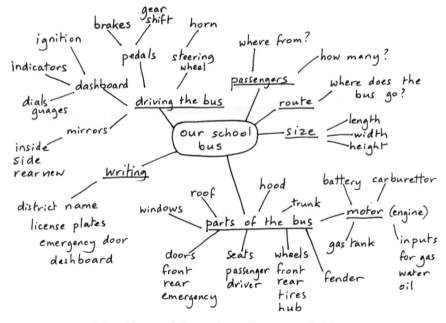

School bus web for a class of younger children.

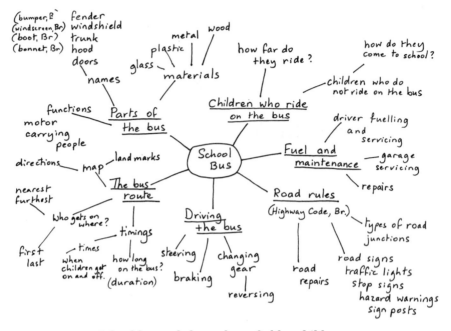

School bus web for a class of older children.

APPENDIX 7

Zoom Web on Homes

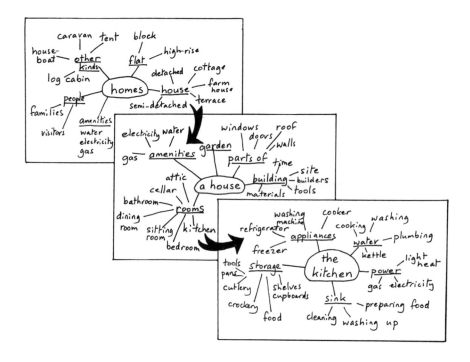

APPENDIX 8

A Walk Around the School[1]

SYLVIA C. CHARD

Teachers can use a walk around the school, or any nature walk, to obtain readily accessible learning materials. Walks can help children take the first important step in learning once they express curiosity. The activities outlined below are not exhaustive. However, they illustrate the principle of relating objects that the children are curious about to the organized disciplines they should begin to master in the school years. The activities are appropriate for children four to eight years of age, although some activities are more appropriate for the older ones.

What to Take Along

Be sure to take sturdy paper bags so that the children can collect rocks, stones, sticks, plants, feathers, bones, insects, or anything else they would like to bring back to look at more closely. In the classroom, some children may wish to pool their collections and work in small groups, while others may prefer to work alone.

The materials collected can be organized to suit various ways of grouping topics and skills. Unlike the way projects are organized in the main part of the book, this outline groups the activities under traditional subject headings reflecting conventional disciplines.

---

[1] Adapted from S. C. Hucklesby [S. C. Chard] (1971), *Opening up the Classroom: A Walk Around the School*. Published by the ERIC Clearinghouse on Early Childhood Education, University of Illinois, Urbana, Illinois.

TEACHING MATHEMATICS WITH ROCKS AND STONES

Mathematics is a good subject to begin with, since there are many ways of using rocks and stones to illustrate or strengthen mathematical concepts. Here are a few starters:

Seriation. Have the children lay out the stones in order of size (e.g., smallest to largest), weight (lightest to heaviest), color (lightest to darkest), shape (flattest to roundest, thinnest to thickest).

Counting. Separate stones into sets by color or size and put each set on separate paper plates. Count the number of stones on each plate, and make a card for each plate showing the number of stones. Talk about how shepherds used "counting stones" to keep track of their sheep.

Weighing. Compare weight of rocks or stones to other ones and to materials such as wood, sand, water, or metal objects. Determine how many smaller stones or rocks it will take to balance a larger one.

Estimating. Try to guess or predict from their size how many stones it might take to fill up a glass jar or to make a stone "path" from one corner of the room to the other. Have the children check their estimates with the facts.

Measuring. Use a tape measure to determine the length, breadth, and circumference of different rocks. Talk about the "stone" as an old unit of measurement. Make a crayon mark on a large stone, roll it along the floor, and count the number of times the mark reappears as a way of describing and measuring the distance covered.

TEACHING SCIENCE WITH STONES

The study of stones and rocks is a natural jumping-off place for introducing the natural and life sciences. Here are some preliminary suggestions:

Identification. Look up the names of rocks and stones in a rock book. Make labels when identification has been successful.

Rocks and Water. Suggest some of the following questions for children to explore:

Do rocks sink or float? Which rocks will sink, which will float? Have the children predict and then test their predictions in answering these questions.

How much water does a rock displace? Measure the spillover. Compare the weight of a cup of sand and rock that displaces an amount of water equal to that displaced by the sand.

Notice how shiny the wet rocks are. Why is that so? How does wetness change the color of stones and rocks?

How does water change the shape of stones (as in erosion)?

Rocks and Fire. With tongs, hold a rock in a candle flame. Ask the children beforehand whether some rocks will burn, what color the flame might be, and whether they will turn black and crumble? Experiment with different rocks and note the differences among them.

Rocks and Motion. Discuss ways of moving large rocks (lever, crane, pulley, etc.). Talk about how the pyramids and other ancient buildings were constructed; contrast them with modern building materials and methods. Take opportunities to observe large mechanical cranes and earth-moving equipment.

Geography and Geology. Suggest some of the following points for discussion: What is the earth made of? Talk about different kinds of rocks and how they were formed; the Rocky Mountains; what makes a valley, landslides, riverbeds, waterfalls, erosion; how rocks can give clues about the past (fossils, arrowheads, etc.).

Human Uses for Rocks. Talk about (or suggest projects involving) stone-age tools, making fire with flint, weapons (throwing rocks, arrowheads, slingshots, catapults), building shelters and houses, extracting metals from rocks, coal for power and heat, sand and gravel for roads, precious gems for decoration and jewelry, sculptures, stone fences, chalkboards, stones in fish tanks, plumb line with a stone.

TEACHING LANGUAGE ARTS WITH STONES

Expressions Involving Stones. Start with some of the following expressions, and encourage the children to think of other sayings, stories, and poems about stones and rocks and to make some up:

"A rolling stone gathers no moss."
"People who live in glass houses shouldn't throw stones."
"A stone's throw from here."
"Rock bottom," "stone-cold," "stone-deaf," "heart of stone," "stoned."
Kidney stones, gravel-voiced

Tell the story of "Stone Soup," tell how the little red hen filled the bag with stones to fool the fox, tell about the Gorgon's head, and David and Goliath.

Famous Rocks. Discuss Plymouth Rock, the Rock of Gibraltar,

Stonehenge, Mount Rushmore and the Presidents' faces carved in stone, "Rock of Ages," prehistoric cave paintings.

Creative Activities. Encourage the children to write poems and stories about some aspect of rocks. Make a rock collage (glue the small stones to background painting), paint stones in bright colors, use colored stones as paperweights. Make beetles, ladybugs, or animals from stones with paper, pipe cleaners, etc. Paint faces on stones, make stone prints.

Vocabulary Enrichment. Inspection and comparison of stones provide a good opportunity to increase vocabulary. Describe:

> *Shape:* round, flat, square, angular, triangular, pointed, top, bottom, wide, long.
>
> *Color:* pale, light, dark, speckled, striped.
>
> *Size:* small, tiny, minute, miniscule, big, large, giant-size, wide.
>
> *Weight:* heavy, light, hefty.
>
> *Comparatives:* heavier, longer, lighter than.
>
> *Texture:* hard, soft, rough, smooth, sharp, flaky, crumbly, rounded, jagged.

Encourage the children to feel the rocks in a bag and guess the color as you say, "Find me the white rough rock," "a yellow sharp pointed rock," "a black smooth rock," and so forth.

Movement. Children will generally enjoy these pantomimes:

- falling like a rock
- carrying a heavy bucket of rocks
- moving a big rock by rocking it back and forth
- walking on a rocky riverbed through the water
- walking with rocks in your shoes
- stumbling, slipping, stubbing your toe
- climbing a rock face and feeling for handholds and footholds in a solid rock face.

LEARNING WITH STICKS

The same sorts of activities can be planned around collections of sticks and plants. The brief outlines that follow present only a few suggestions to serve as starting points.

Sticks and Mathematics

Sorting. Lay out sticks according to length, thickness, color, roughness, alive or dead, kind of bush, tree, or plant.

Seriation. Lay out according to length such as stick, rod, pole, log, stakes.

Counting. Make groups and sets by number.

Weighing and Measuring. Estimate lengths of various sticks; talk about use of rods and poles as measuring tools.

Shapes. Make geometric shapes with sticks and lumps of clay.

Sticks and Science

Identify the source of sticks and twigs in a tree book. Suggest questions for the children to explore:
Do sticks burn? green ones too? both when wet and dry? Do sticks float or sink? Does weight make any difference in ability to float? What are differences between green and dead sticks? What are some different qualities of various woods? What happens to trees in winter? Note the way some insects are camouflaged to look like the plants and trees they inhabit. Take a field trip to a tree nursery.

Human Uses for Sticks, Poles, Logs

Many uses can be discussed: starting fires by rubbing sticks together; burning in fires for heat, power, cooking. Early writing by making pictures in the sand and dirt. Fishing rods, bows and arrows, boomerangs, spears, house frames, teepees, hammocks, birch canoes, propulsion of boats with oars and poles, masts, rafts, fences, stilts, flagpoles, totem poles, handles of tools, brooms as little sticks fastened to a big one, divining rod for water detection, beating drums.

Sticks and Art

Use sticks to apply paint or scratch designs in paint or crayon. Use in printing. Make collages. Make models with sticks and clay, sticks and paper (kites), sticks and cloth (teepee, hammock, wagon cover), sticks and sand (walls of a fort). Draw stick men and women.

Sticks and Music

Sticks can be struck against one another, used for drumsticks, hollowed for pipes, used to clean flutes. Sounds that sticks make include scraping, grating, creaking, snapping, cracking.

Similar activities can be developed with other materials gathered on the walk. For example, with leaves and flowers, the teacher can develop groups of activities and explorations under the general headings of language arts, mathematics, science, human uses, art, music, movement, and creative writing.

APPENDIX 9

Project Web for "How We Get Our Fish"

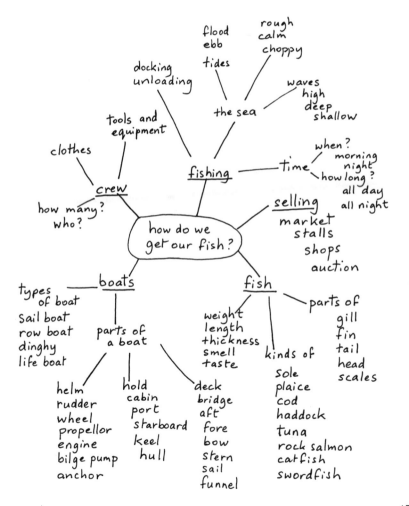

APPENDIX 10

A Check List for Recording Missouri State Competencies Applied in the Course of Project Work

DESIGNED BY DR. FAY MOORE[1]
William Jewell College
Liberty, Missouri

The first page consists of a matrix formed by combining the Missouri State Competencies with the activities included in a project.

At the top of the matrix page the teacher indicates the theme or name of the project and the name of the child whose activities are to be recorded.

The left-hand column, entitled "Core Competencies," corresponds to the attached list of Missouri competencies. The alphabetical listing on the matrix corresponds to the letters under each heading on the Missouri competency list.

A check mark can be entered in the cell if the competency is addressed by the activity. A circle can be drawn around the check mark when the child completes the activity.

---

[1]Reproduced by permission of the author.

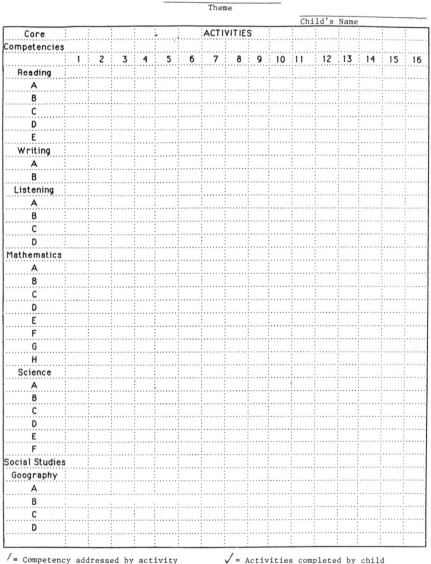

/ = Competency addressed by activity   √ = Activities completed by child

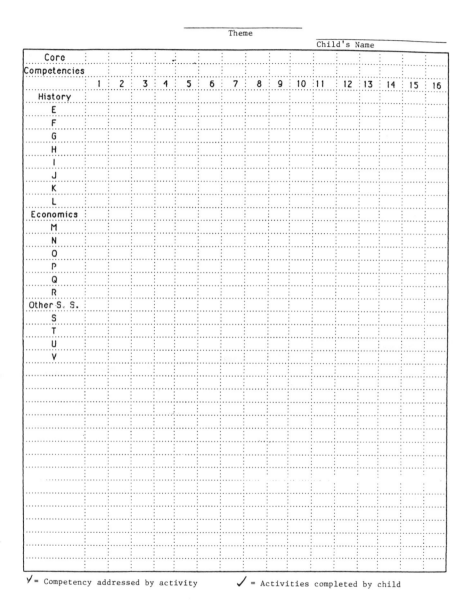

Theme

Child's Name

Core Competencies	1	2	3	4	5	6	7	8	9	10	11	12	13	14	15	16
History																
E																
F																
G																
H																
I																
J																
K																
L																
Economics																
M																
N																
O																
P																
Q																
R																
Other S. S.																
S																
T																
U																
V																

ᵛ = Competency addressed by activity   ✓ = Activities completed by child

MISSOURI COMPETENCIES—LEVEL 1

Reading

A.   Use appropriate letter-sound, structural and contextual strategies to determine identification of unknown words.
B.   Demonstrate the ability to determine the meaning of unknown words in context.
C.   Recognize or demonstrate an understanding of narrative and expository text by retelling, answering or formulating questions and thinking critically.
D.   Employ appropriate strategies for locating and using information.
E.   Apply reading for personal development.

Writing

A.   Use the tools or means for writing. (Penmanship)
B.   Use steps of the writing process: prewriting, composing, revising, proofing/editing, sharing the product.

Listening/Speakinng

A.   Listen attentively and critically.
B.   Use conventions of oral language.
C.   Organize thoughts, ideas and materials for listening and speaking.
D.   Use and respond to verbal and nonverbal communication.

Mathematics

A.   Demonstrate an understanding of numbers.
B.   Apply the basic operations in computational situations.
C.   Estimate results and judge reasonableness of solutions.
D.   Apply the concept of measurement to the physical world.
E.   Recognize geometric relationships.
F.   Use statistical techniques and interpret statistical information.
G.   Apply problem-solving strategies.
H.   Solve problems in consumer situations.

Science

A.   Observe by using the five senses the properties of objects, organisms and events.

B. Classify by grouping objects or events into categories according to similarities or differences.
C. Measure matter, energy, space and time.
D. Communicate observations or findings by describing, drawing, recording data and graphing.
E. Infer by forming guess(es) from observations or findings.
F. Predict by forecasting future events or conditions based upon past observations or inferences.

Social Studies/Civics

Geography
A. Demonstrate knowledge of place geography.
B. Demonstrate an understanding of relationships between people and their surroundings.
C. Demonstrate an understanding of spatial relationships.
D. Use map-reading and map-making skills.

History/Government
E. Demonstrate knowledge of significant historical events and developments, their relationships to each other and to the present.
F. Understand how people's positions and experiences influence their views of events.
G. Understand and apply basic principles of our political system.
H. Understand basic institutions and processes of law making, law enforcement and law interpretation.
I. Understand rights and responsibilities of citizens in democratic societies.
J. Understand processes by which citizens may help resolve disputes and influence policy making.
K. Analyze real and hypothetical cases in relation to persistent issues of government in American society.
L. Apply analytic skills to political messages and discussions.

Economics
M. Analyze economic decision situations with awareness of opportunity costs and trade-offs.
N. Understand factors of production, their interrelationships and how investment in them relates to productivity.
O. Understand economic relationships (flow of money, goods and services) among households, businesses, financial institutions, labor unions and government in this and other economic systems.
P. Understand relationships among supply, demand, price and quantity of goods and services.

Q. Understand how a nation's level of output, income, employment and distribution of income is determined.

R. Understand principles related to trade (personal, regional or international).

Other Social Studies

S. Understand cause-and-effect relationships related to the behavior of individuals and groups.

T. Understand institutions and processes for meeting basic human needs.

U. Understand variations among cultures in their belief systems, institutions and social structures.

V. Understand and use appropriate techniques for investigating social studies topics.

Author Index

Subject Index